CAREERS IN DEMAND
FOR HIGH SCHOOL GRADUATES

Computers, Communications & the Arts

Daniel Lewis

MASON CREST

Mason Crest
450 Parkway Drive, Suite D
Broomall, PA 19008
www.masoncrest.com

Printed in the United States of America
First printing
9 8 7 6 5 4 3 2 1

Series ISBN: 978-1-4222-4132-5
Hardcover ISBN: 978-1-4222-4134-9

Library of Congress Cataloging-in-Publication Data is available on file.

Developed and Produced by Print Matters Productions, Inc.
(www.printmattersinc.com)
Cover and Interior Design by Lori S Malkin Design, LLC

CAREERS IN DEMAND FOR
HIGH SCHOOL GRADUATES

Agriculture, Food & Natural Resourccs

Armed Forces

Computers, Communications & the Arts

Construction & Trades

Fitness, Personal Care Services & Education

Health Care & Science

Hospitality & Human Services

Public Safety & Law

Sales, Marketing & Finance

Transportation & Manufacturing

KEY ICONS TO LOOK FOR:

 Words to understand: These words with their easy-to-understand definitions will increase the reader's understanding of the text while building vocabulary skills.

 Sidebars: This boxed material within the main text allows readers to build knowledge, gain insights, explore possibilities, and broaden their perspectives by weaving together additional information to provide realistic and holistic perspectives.

 Educational Videos: Readers can view videos by scanning our QR codes, providing them with additional educational content to supplement the text. Examples include news coverage, moments in history, speeches, iconic sports moments and much more!

 Text-dependent Questions: These questions send the reader back to the text for more careful attention to the evidence presented there.

 Research projects: Readers are pointed toward areas of further inquiry connected to each chapter. Suggestions are provided for projects that encourage deeper research and analysis.

CONTENTS

For millions of Americans, life after high school means stepping into the real world. Each year more than 1 million of the nation's 3.1 million high school graduates go directly into the workforce. Clearly, college isn't for everyone. Many people learn best by using their hands rather than by sitting in a classroom. Others find that the escalating cost of college puts it beyond reach, at least for the time being. During the 2016–2017 school year, for instance, tuition and fees at a "moderate" four-year, in-state public college averaged $24,610, not including housing costs, according to The College Board.

The good news is that there's a wide range of exciting, satisfying careers available without a four-year bachelor's degree or even a two-year associate's degree. Careers in Demand for High School Graduates highlights specific, in-demand careers in which individuals who have only a high school diploma or the general educational development (GED) credential can find work, with or without further training (outside of college).

These jobs span the range from apprentice electronics technician to chef, teacher's assistant, Web page designer, sales associate, and lab technician. The additional training that some of these positions require may be completed either on the job, through a certificate program, or during an apprenticeship that combines entry-level work and class time. Happily, there's plenty of growth in the number of jobs that don't require a college diploma, though that growth is fastest for positions that call for additional technical training or a certificate of proficiency.

So what career should a high school graduate consider? The range is so broad that Careers in Demand for High School Graduates includes 10 volumes, each based on related career fields from the Department of Labor's career clusters. Within each volume approximately 10 careers are profiled, encouraging readers to focus on a wide selection of job possibilities, some of which readers may not even know exist. To enable readers to narrow their choices, each chapter offers a self-assessment quiz that helps answer the question, "Is this career for me?" What's more, each job profile includes an insightful look at what the position involves, highlights of a typical day, insight into the work environment, and an interview with someone on the job.

An essential part of the decision to enter a particular field includes how much additional training is needed. Careers in Demand features opportunities that require no further academic study or training beyond high school as well as those that do. Readers in high school can start prepping for careers immediately through volunteer work, internships, academic classes, technical programs, or

▲ A computer support desk specialist needs to be good with computers and enjoy helping people.

career academies. (Currently, for instance, one in four students concentrates on a vocational or technical program.) For each profile, the best ways for high school students to prepare are featured in a "Start Preparing Now" section.

For readers who are called to serve in the armed forces, this decision also provides an opportunity to step into a range of careers. Every branch of the armed forces, from the army to the coast guard, offers training in areas including administrative, construction, electronics, health care, and protective services. One volume of Careers in Demand for High School Graduates is devoted to careers that can be reached with military training. These range from personnel specialist to aircraft mechanic.

Beyond military options, other entry-level careers provide job seekers with an opportunity to test-drive a career without a huge commitment. Compare the ease of switching from being a bank teller to a sales representative, for instance, with that of investing three years and tens of thousands of dollars into a law school education, only to discover a dislike for the profession. This series offers not only a look at related careers, but also ways to advance in the field. Another section, "Finding a Job," provides job-hunting tips specific to each career. This includes, for instance, advice for teacher assistants to develop a portfolio of their work. As it turns out, employers of entry-level workers aren't looking for degrees and academic achievements. They want employability skills: a sense of responsibility, a willingness to learn, discipline, flexibility, and above all, enthusiasm. Luckily, with 100 jobs profiled in Careers in Demand for High School Graduates, finding the perfect one to get enthusiastic about is easier than ever.

TV/Film Camera Operator

1

Help create TV shows and movies. Make a living doing something you love. Work in an exciting industry.

WORDS TO UNDERSTAND

freelancer: a person who works for a variety of companies rather than being tied to one.

networking: meeting people in a particular field to gain contacts and information.

predominant: the most frequent or common.

proficiency: degree of skill in a particular activity.

Americans watch four and five hours of TV every day and spend an average of 10 hours at the movies each year. Yet some of the most important people in the TV and film industry are never seen on camera—because they're the ones running the camera itself! TV and film camera operators are in charge of capturing the action in front of the camera, no matter whether it's actors performing parts in a movie or real-life happenings, such as professional sports, news events, and interviews for documentaries. Other TV and film camera operators work shooting everything from soap commercials to wars. There are about 21,700 TV and film camera operators working today in the United States.

◀ There are thousands of TV and film camera operators in the United States, and there is plenty of work filming outdoor scenes.

Is This Job Right for You?

To find out if being a TV or film camera operator is right for you, read each of the following questions and answer "Yes" or "No."

Yes	No	1.	*Are you a team player?*
Yes	No	2.	*Do you have a good artistic "eye?"*
Yes	No	3.	*Do you take directions well?*
Yes	No	4.	*Are you good with technology?*
Yes	No	5.	*Are you physically strong?*
Yes	No	6.	*Can you work long or irregular hours?*
Yes	No	7.	*Do you work well under pressure?*
Yes	No	8.	*Are you willing to start at the bottom?*
Yes	No	9.	*Can you move to where a job is, if necessary?*
Yes	No	10.	*Do you have good communications skills?*

If you answered "Yes" to most of these questions, you may have the essential skills for a career as a TV or film camera operator. To find out more about this job, read on.

What's the Work Like?

The TV or film camera operator's job starts long before the director calls "Action!" Much of the magic of show business is planning—positioning the cameras, getting the lighting just right, and deciding when you'll be zooming in for a close-up and when you'll be pulling back for a long shot. You'll be working closely with the director, the sound and light equipment operators, and the "talent"—the people who will appear on camera. Of course, that's only if you're working in a studio. The places where a TV or film camera operator might work are as varied as the places where exciting and interesting things happen. You might find yourself doing everything from covering the opening of a new mini-mall to running through a war zone.

One thing doesn't change, though: The job of the TV or film camera operator is to capture images. In order to do this, you'll need a good sense of timing, as well as

TALKING MONEY

Employment in all media occupations is expected to continue to grow at a rate of about 4 percent. It's important to be aware, however, that there is a lot of competition for jobs in this high-stress and demanding, yet very desirable, industry.

▲ The film industry can take you to many different places, including the beach. Be sure to dress appropriately as you'll have to work through varied weather conditions too.

good hand–eye coordination to operate the camera. You'll also need to pay attention to the instructions of the director and the producer. They will have very clear ideas of what they want the finished product to look like, and it's your job to help them accomplish this.

TV and film camera operators use many different kinds of cameras, from small handheld cameras to large ones mounted on crane arms. In the past few years, digital cameras have become **predominant** in most situations. Digital video is not only easier to edit but can save money by not needing film, which is expensive both to buy and develop. They also tend to be smaller and easier to carry. What this means is that TV and film camera operators will have to be comfortable with computers and digital editing programs.

Who's Hiring?

- TV production companies

- Movie studios

- Local TV stations

- Production companies

TALKING TRENDS

The median income for TV or film camera operators is $63,020 per year but can vary between $26,940 and $109,200, depending on your seniority and who you work for. Many are **freelancers** whose earnings change considerably from year to year.

Where Are the Jobs?

The largest numbers of openings for TV and film camera operator jobs are in Los Angeles or New York, since these cities are where most movies, television shows, and commercials are shot. However, there are openings everywhere, since local TV news always needs camera operators. Major news organizations are also based in other cities. CNN, for instance, is headquartered in Atlanta, Georgia. TV commercials are also shot around the country.

The hours and workplaces for a TV or film camera operator can be very irregular. While TV and film camera operators employed by TV stations, called *studio camera operators,* usually work five-day, 40-hour weeks, this can vary widely depending on production schedules. Film camera operators, also called *cinematographers,* may have to travel widely to shoot on location. They may work 12- to 14-hour days on one project for weeks on end, and then have

▲ News camera operators can be called upon to broadcast from virtually anywhere in the world.

▲ Cameras vary in size. Some are small and nearly handheld while others are the size of one's body and much heavier.

NOTES FROM THE FIELD

TV camera operator, *Minneapolis, Minnesota*

Q: *How did you get your job?*

A: It's all about networking, knowing people who know people and making sure the people who hire crews know who you are. Volunteering for cable access or something like a large megaplex church that does a lot of video is a good way to meet people who may have connections that will get you an entry-level position on a crew somewhere. Internships don't really get you working on a TV crew, in my experience, since they're mostly geared toward four-year-degree-in-journalism types who want to produce or appear on camera.

Q: *What do you like best about your job?*

A: The challenge, the creativity, and the feeling you get when you're working on a live production that flows absolutely smoothly because you're working with a great team of professionals. If you're a musician, it's a feeling akin to taking part in a great improvised jam session, only much more expensive.

Q: *What's the most challenging part of your job?*

A: It's a 10-hour day, minimum. On your feet, lots of lifting and carrying. The pressure, too—it's live television, so there are no do-overs. Either you get it right the first time or people know you screwed up. People at home may not know it's you personally, but the person who hired you sure will. That's why you have to spend a lot of time working your way up, because when a million people are watching you, there can't be any possibility of a mistake.

Q: *What are the keys to success as a TV or film camera operator?*

A: Common sense, people skills, networking, creativity, intimate familiarity with the sport or other subject matter you're shooting. Actual technical proficiency at running the equipment pretty much takes care of itself through the practice you get in the process of working your way up. You won't get hired for bigger gigs until you demonstrate your proficiency on smaller ones.

no work for a month or two. News camera operators, also called *electronic news gathering (ENG) operators,* may have to be available on short notice to fly to distant places. They may have to quickly edit their footage themselves for immediate broadcast. Their work can also be dangerous, especially if they cover wars or natural disasters.

The sorts of cameras used by people in this profession vary widely. You might have a camera light enough to be carried in one hand, or one that you need a crane to move. Some TV and film camera operators use specialized cameras, such as Steadicams (made by Tiffen) and those used to shoot special effects or animation.

Start Preparing Now

- Assemble a "reel," or sample tape, of work you've done. This can showcase your shooting and editing skills.

- Volunteer or intern. This will help you meet people who can help you get entry-level jobs.

- Take classes. There are many filmmaking programs, and though you don't need a formal degree to be a camera operator, employers may want to know that you know what you're doing.

A Typical Day

Here are the highlights of a typical day for a TV or film camera operator.

Start early. Your phone rings at 5 a.m. A client you worked for last month is shooting a TV commercial today, and the regular camera operator is sick. Are you interested in some work? Oh, yes— you have an hour to get to the set.

Hurry up and wait. The talent doesn't have to be on the set until 10 a.m., but you've already spent the past four hours setting up the cameras. Unfortunately, this is a diaper commercial, which means the "talent" is a pair of two-year-old twin girls—which means you have to wait around while the director gets them just in the right spot, tries to get them to smile, or swaps them when they begin crying or need a diaper change.

Finish late. Long after the talent goes home, you're still at work, spending hours getting shot after shot of a box of diapers for the commercial. You leave work exhausted—but with a large paycheck!

Training and How to Get It

Though you don't need a college degree to be a TV or film camera operator, training never hurts. Many high schools have audiovisual clubs and video labs that you can practice with. Also consider getting a camera and some editing software to practice on your own—and keep in mind that if you have a phone, you already own a pretty decent camera. You can also read trade magazines to learn the latest techniques and tips.

Another way to learn the basics is through an entry-level job, summer employment, or an internship. There you will learn to set up lights and shots, make adjustments to cameras, and decide what to photograph. There are also many filmmaking schools that can teach you the basics of the trade—everything from lighting and setting up shots to developing the finished film. Such schools can be expensive, however, and completing a course is no guarantee of getting a job.

Since computers are becoming more and more important in the TV and film industries, it is important to be computer literate. Learn to use editing software, and also learn how digital video is different from analog and from the various film stocks. Things can look very different on a computer than they do projected on a movie screen.

▲ Film editing is nearly all digital so you need to be familiar with the major editing programs.

Finally, some of the things employers look for in a TV or film camera operator, such as a good artistic eye, creativity, and imagination, can't be taught. However, you need to be able to demonstrate these attributes. To this end, you should get as much practice as you can, and prepare a videotape or DVD of your work to show prospective employers.

See what it's like to be a camera operator.

Learn the Lingo

Here are a few words you'll hear as a TV or film camera operator:

- **Steadicam** Unlike other cameras, the Tiffen Steadicam is mounted on a harness. A special arm keeps it from shaking as the operator moves, resulting in a smooth shot.

- **Editor** The editor is the person who takes the raw footage shot by the camera operator and puts it together to tell a story.

- **ENG** (electronic news gathering). Industry shorthand for a sole reporter or a whole crew who transmit their stories via radio waves to the broadcast production studio.

Finding a Job

As has often been said, it's not just what you know, but who you know. The most important consideration employers look for in the TV and film industries is reputation. Reputation comes from people both knowing your work and knowing you as an experienced and reliable camera operator. If you want to work as a TV or film camera operator, then you should start making contacts in the industry right away. The people you meet may be able to get you jobs later on.

The other factor in the equation is experience. However, people who work for the TV and film industries tend to be film buffs and video "junkies" from a young age, and there are many ways for creative people to get experience: Start a public-access TV show with some friends. Work on an independent movie, or even make your own. Volunteer at a church or organization that does a lot of video work and look for summer jobs and internships. All of these are also good ways to meet people who can help you find jobs. Moreover, by giving expression to your creative energies, you can learn to become a skilled camera operator.

Tips for Success

- Pay attention to directions. Remember, you're part of a team.

- Be a people person. TV and film are highly social industries.

- Consider moving to where the work is. There are more jobs in film and TV in big cities than there are in small towns.

LEARN MORE ONLINE

NATIONAL ASSOCIATION OF BROADCAST EMPLOYEES AND TECHNICIANS
This is the union for TV camera operators and other professionals. http://www.nabetcwa.org

INTERNATIONAL CINEMATOGRAPHER'S GUILD
This is the international union for people who operate cameras for movies, and the Web site features technical tips. http://www.cameraguild.com

Reality Check

The TV and film industries are highly competitive. This means that not only is it difficult to get jobs, but because many TV and film camera operators are freelancers, you may go a long time between jobs.

Related Jobs to Consider

Set dresser. When you've watched two people having dinner in a movie, have you ever wondered who put the plates on the tables? Guess what—it's the set dresser. This is one of the many behind-the-scenes jobs in the movie industry.

Sound technician. Sound technicians are to the ear what camera operators are to the eye. They are responsible for capturing the audio portion of the film or TV show.

Lighting technician. Cameras don't work unless they have light! Also, the quality of light can make a big difference in the finished product. The lighter's job is to make sure that everybody looks perfect.

How to Move Up

- Go big. Successful camera operators can move to bigger and bigger jobs. Eventually they can earn administrative positions, such as directors of photography.

- Those who can, teach. If you're a successful camera operator, why not get a job at a technical school teaching other people to become camera operators?

- Become a director. Consider making your own independent films and documentaries.

TEXT-DEPENDENT QUESTIONS

1. *What is the median income for camera operators?*

2. *What is a "reel" and why do you need one?*

3. *What does a set dresser do?*

4. *What are the unions that many camera operators join?*

RESEARCH PROJECTS

1. *Make your own reel. Remember, you don't need lots of high-tech gear to gain experience as a camera operator: just use your phone! If you are interested in TV news, take your phone to a school event and try your hand at shooting and editing a "story" about what happens there. If Hollywood is more appealing, get in touch with the drama club at your school—chances are they would love to have someone film a production or even just a rehearsal.*

2. *Read this article about the daily life of a camera operator for the sports network ESPN. Consider if this sounds like the type of day you'd like to have. (http://www.espn.com/espnw/athletes-life/article/14474327/scenes-tv-camera-operator-elaine-rom)*

Grip, Stagehand, Set-Up Worker

2

Help to make films, television shows, and dramatic productions. Work in an exciting industry. Meet interesting people.

WORDS TO UNDERSTAND

advent: the arrival of a particular event or trend.

boom mic: a microphone attached to a long pole.

diffuses: spreads over a large area.

internship: a low-level assistant or trainee job, usually taken to gain experience.

irregular: unpredictable.

When you watch a movie or TV show or go to a play or rock concert, all you usually see are the actors or musicians. Behind the scenes, dozens or even hundreds of people have worked hard to make what you see possible. Grips, stagehands, and set-up workers do everything needed in a stage or screen production, from placing the lights and holding the **boom mics** on a TV show to changing the scenery in an opera or making sure that a sound stage set up to look like a diner has plates and napkins. The total number of people who work in these types of jobs is not easy to pin down. However, the International Union of Theatrical and Stage Employees (IATSE) has more than 130,000 members in the United States, and many more people work in these jobs in a nonunion capacity.

◀ Stagehands work behind the scenes to make sure that each concert or play goes smoothly.

◀ The boom mic is very important in film and television as it allows an actor to move about freely without disturbing the sound.

Is This Job Right for You?

To find out if being a grip, stagehand, or set-up worker is right for you, read each of the following questions and answer "Yes" or "No."

Yes	No	1.	*Can you move to where a job is, if necessary?*
Yes	No	2.	*Can you work long or irregular hours?*
Yes	No	3.	*Do you take directions well?*
Yes	No	4.	*Are you very organized?*
Yes	No	5.	*Are you physically strong?*
Yes	No	6.	*Do you have a good creative "eye?"*
Yes	No	7.	*Do you work well under pressure?*
Yes	No	8.	*Are you willing to start at the bottom?*
Yes	No	9.	*Are you a team player?*
Yes	No	10.	*Do you have good communications skills?*

If you answered "Yes" to most of these questions, you might be right for a career as a grip, stagehand, or set-up worker. To find out more about these jobs, read on.

What's the Work Like?

Grips, stagehands, and set-up workers do everything that is not acting, directing, production, or another specialized skill, such as using a camera.

Grips work in movies. They cooperate closely with both the lighting and camera departments to make sure the cameras are in place and the lights are set up. On union jobs, grips do not touch the cameras or lights themselves, but they do everything else that will handle how the light **diffuses** across the set.

Stagehands work in theater. They may find themselves working in lights, sound, operating the *fly system* as part of the fly crew, or a number of other jobs.

Set-up workers may find themselves anywhere from marking the places where the actors will stand to rigging heavy lights hundreds of feet above the ground. In large production houses, responsibilities are carefully defined. For instance, suppose a scene calls for a sword fight to break out on the deck of a ship between two actors playing pirates. *Wardrobe* will handle the pirate costumes, *property* will handle the swords and everything an actor will touch, use, or carry, while a *set dresser* will set up all the background props, such as ropes, rigging, belaying pins, and cannonballs. The *swing gang* makes last-minute changes to the set before filming, such as moving a cannon that is interfering with the camera.

Who's Hiring?

- TV production companies

- Movie studios

- Local TV stations

- Production companies

- Theaters and theater companies

- Musicians and touring companies

▲ Roadies are in charge of moving and setting up lights and other equipment touring productions or bands.

Where Are the Jobs?

Many openings for grips, stagehands, and set-up workers are in Los Angeles or New York, since these cities both have large theater scenes and because many movies, television shows, and commercials are shot there. Grips, stagehands, and set-up workers usually work in theaters, studios, and sound stages, but for filming on location, you may need to travel to distant parts of the country or the world. Some jobs are exclusively on the road. For instance, *roadies* go along with a touring production or band to do their set-up for them in various venues.

Hours in the entertainment industry can be very irregular, with 14- to 18-hour days one month followed by several weeks of unemployment. Because of this, it can be difficult to estimate what your earnings will be for a particular year. On the other hand, if you are working for certain productions, such as a Broadway show, you might have a fairly regular work schedule. The motion picture industry, in general, tends to provide more irregular work than is found with regular live productions.

See what it's like to work as a grip.

Some of the work can be strenuous or dangerous, such as rigging lights high off the ground, but the danger you will be exposed to is usually limited by contract. Employers in the entertainment industry are required to take care of their employees' well-being.

▲ Prepping for a show can be exhausting and strenuous. There are trunks and trunks full of equipment to be prepped and staged before a show starts. Then, it all needs to be broken down and packed back up at the end of the night.

A Typical Day

Here are the highlights of a typical day for a set-up worker.

Up at dawn. Today you'll be working in the property department of the new pirate film *Swashbucklers of the Sargasso*. The call is for 6 a.m., which means that you're dressed and out of your hotel room before the sun is up.

Set it up . . . and set it up again. Your job doesn't end after you hand the actors their prop swords and set up the pirate ship to look like it's from the 1700s. The director wants take after take, and after each, you need to restack the cannonballs, make sure the rigging's tight, and everything's generally shipshape. In the meantime, you wait around for when you're needed.

Break it down. The scene finally finishes shooting around 11 p.m., but your day's not over—you still have to put away all those cannonballs!

Start Preparing Now

- Get to know people. The entertainment industry is a very social one, and contacts you make now can help you later on.

- Work in school productions and amateur theater. Do everything you can to gain experience.

- Study everything you can about how movies and TV shows are filmed.

NOTES FROM THE FIELD

Set-up worker, *Los Angeles, California*

Q: *How did you get your job?*

A: I initially started working at Roger Corman doing Craft Service, meaning I bought all the snacks for the crew. It was the only job I could get that paid money that was actually in film production. The film industry is notorious for nonpaying internships. I eventually landed in Property, which is basically anything the actor handles, your department is responsible for.

Q: *What do you like best about your job?*

A: I love the variety of people I have met in the film industry. Every type of person you could possibly imagine is in some way or another incorporated into the film industry on some level. It's a very dynamic community.

Q: *What's the most challenging part of your job?*

A: The most challenging part of my job is probably the schedule and the hours. I have worked both a lot of television and film, and it's not uncommon to work a 16-hour day. Once in a while is not that bad, but try doing it every day for a few weeks, and you know what true exhaustion is. I'm pregnant with my first child right now, and I'm trying to figure out how to juggle work and family life. My husband is a special effects engineer and cameraman, and he travels a lot. It's not unusual for him to be on location for six months at a time. I have stayed closer to home because I have worked more on television series the past four years.

Q: *What are the keys to success as a grip, stagehand, or set-up worker?*

A: Personally, I think everybody has their own path to success, and don't listen too much what other people tell you are the secrets. What works for one person isn't going to necessarily work for another. You do need to be dedicated to what you do, and that goes for anything. I don't think that's a secret. Plus, it's always easier to be dedicated to something that you love.

Training and How to Get It

Most grips, stagehands, and set-up workers are trained informally on the job. This is definitely an industry where you learn by doing and where experience counts. For this reason, it is best to get as much experience as possible. Try to join community theater or independent movie productions. There are also film schools that can teach you some of the basics of the motion picture industry. Such schools can be expensive, however, and completing a course is no guarantee of getting a job.

Another way to learn the basics is through an entry-level job, summer employment, or an internship. There you will learn to set up lights and scenery, handle equipment, make scene changes, and do everything else that a grip, stagehand, or set-up worker does.

▲ A scrim is often used in film and television industries to control the quality of the light.

Learn the Lingo

Here are a few words you'll hear as a grip, stagehand, or set-up worker:

- **Cutting light** To "cut" light is to focus, refract, reflect, or diffuse it so that a scene is lit exactly the way it should be.

- **Fly system** The system of weights and pulleys used to raise and lower scenery and other items in a theatrical production.

- **Prop** Short for "theatrical property"—the physical objects that actors interact with. Often humorously defined as anything that gets in your way during a scene change. This may include actors.

Finding a Job

In the entertainment industry everyone needs friends, and grips, stagehands, and set-up workers are no exceptions. Knowing people in the industry can help you find openings and, more importantly, get you hired. The best way to meet people, of course, is to work in the industry. This is why **internships** and volunteer experience can be so important—they show that you know what you're doing. To find a position, ask local production companies and theater groups if they need any workers.

You can often find paying jobs for grips, stagehands, and set-up workers advertised in newspapers, free weeklies, and trade publications. Look also on Web sites such as Craigslist (http://www.craigs list.org) or Variety.com.

While getting your foot in the door is important, it is your reputation that will get you more work. People in charge of productions want to know that they can count on you. Always be sure to do a good job, and you can count on recommendations and references later on.

Tips for Success

- Pay attention! Things can happen quickly. You should be changing the scenery or handing the prop to the actor before the director even asks you.

- Do a thorough job. Everything you do contributes to the overall quality of the performance.

Reality Check

Grips, stagehands, and set-up workers do all the heavy, unglamorous work in theater. The work can be stressful and the salary **irregular**. However, you do get to work in an exciting, creative environment.

Related Jobs to Consider

Set decorator or props person. Instead of moving the scenery and props, why not make them?

Camera operator. Camera operators are an important part of shooting any film or TV program.

Electrician. Why not learn to operate the lights instead of setting them up? Electricians are the ones in charge of the lights themselves, and as union members, they have more job security.

How to Move Up

- Become a designer. Many stage designers started on the bottom as stagehands.

- Become a director. Give expression to your own creative energies.

- Learn a trade. Skilled workers, such as carpenters and electricians, are indispensable to theatrical production.

LEARN MORE ONLINE

LIFE AS A STAGEHAND
Read one man's tale of life behind the scenes.
http://www.flyingmoose.org/stage/stage.htm

IATSE 80
The Motion Picture Studio Grips' Union. http://www.iatselocal80.org

TEXT-DEPENDENT QUESTIONS

1. *What are some examples of places where stagehands work?*

2. *What does a grip do?*

3. *What does "cutting light" mean?*

4. *How might you move up in this career?*

RESEARCH PROJECTS

1. *Find out where your local theater group produces their shows and introduce yourself to their technical director. Find out what training he or she has, and ask if you can help out on the next production.*

2. *Look at the listings in Variety (careers.variety.com) and see what types of jobs are available in your area or in an area where you'd like to live. Consider if the jobs sound appealing to you. What kinds of requirements do they have?*

Photographer's Assistant

3

Meet creative people. Work in an exciting industry. See your work in print.

WORDS TO UNDERSTAND

archive: a collection of historical documents.

diffused: spread over a large area.

internship: a low-level assistant or trainee job, usually taken to gain experience.

portfolio: here, a collection of creative work that shows off the artist's skills.

valet: a personal attendant.

Louis Daguerre's invention of practical photography in 1826 gave rise to a whole new art form. Soon photography was replacing painting as the way people wanted to have their portraits made, how they remembered the past, and how they saw the world. With the advent of new printing methods in the 20th century, photographs could easily and cheaply be printed in books and magazines, and photography became an even bigger business. Today photographers do everything from taking baby pictures at shopping malls to shooting supermodels in the latest fashions. Photographer's assistants help photographers in all they do, from carrying equipment to setting up lights to working with models. Usually, photographer's assistants are aspiring photographers themselves. There are about 125,000 professional photographers working in this highly competitive field in the United States today.

◀ As a photographer's assistant you may find yourself carrying equipment, reloading cameras, or even fixing a model's hair for the perfect shot.

Is This Job Right for You?

To find out if being a photographer's assistant is right for you, read each of the following questions and answer "Yes" or "No."

Yes	No	1.	*Do you love photography?*
Yes	No	2.	*Do you work well with all sorts of people?*
Yes	No	3.	*Do you have an artistic eye for color and light?*
Yes	No	4.	*Can you carry heavy loads?*
Yes	No	5.	*Are you very patient?*
Yes	No	6.	*Are you good with computers and technology?*
Yes	No	7.	*Do you pay attention to details?*
Yes	No	8.	*Are you knowledgeable about photography equipment?*
Yes	No	9.	*Can you follow directions?*
Yes	No	10.	*Do you mind starting at the bottom?*

If you answered "Yes" to most of these questions, you may have the talent to pursue a career as a photographer's assistant. To find out more about this job, read on.

What's the Work Like?

Since photographer's assistants tend to be aspiring photographers themselves, they should know the elements of photography. Most important is good light. To achieve a certain look, a photographer may need a certain sort of light, such as a **diffused** glow or a spotlight that casts strong shadows. A large part of the photographer's assistant's job is setting up lights. The photographer's assistant should know—or be willing to learn—how to set up light boxes, lamps, reflectors, and other equipment to achieve these effects, as well as how to use light meters. Part of the job also includes carrying and connecting transformers and generators for the lights, as well as other equipment.

TALKING MONEY

The U.S. Department of Labor does not keep statistics on photographer's assistants, but the median annual income for salaried photographers is $34,070 and ranges from $9.19 to $36.65 per hour. News organizations and scientific companies tend to pay at the higher end of the scale. Photographer's assistants tend to make much less. In fact, many work as volunteers or as part of an **internship** in order to gain experience.

◄ The glare of sunlight can interfere with an outdoor photo shoot. Reflectors can be used to control the light in these situations.

Being organized is also very important. During a shoot, you will hand cameras to the photographer, change the film in cameras, put spent film into canisters, and mark down what is on the film. For larger shoots, you might do anything and everything needed. For instance, you may coordinate schedules with hairdressers and costumers, tell models when they are needed on the set, take care of paperwork, make sure releases are signed, and arrange catering. You might even videotape the proceedings. If you assist a photographer who works in news media, you will not work in such a controlled environment. You may have to carry heavy equipment for long distances. You may also have to travel to distant or even dangerous locations.

Finally, you should remember that, as an assistant, you may be doing a lot of things that aren't in your literal job description. Especially in high-living places like New York, photographer's assistants tend to become all-around **valets**. You might find yourself picking up dry cleaning as well as loading film. In exchange for your labor, though, you should be learning the art of photography in an exciting and creative environment. However, keep in mind that where you intern affects where you find work: If you intern in the New York fashion industry, then that is where your contacts will be.

Who's Hiring?

- Freelance photographers

- Photography studios

- News organizations

Where Are the Jobs?

Photographer's assistants sometimes have the luxury of working in comfortable, well-lit, and climate-controlled studios. However, you may have to travel to all sorts of interesting sites, including showrooms, dance clubs, or tropical islands. A fine art photographer might shoot pictures of animals in a zoo or bodybuilders in the gym—anywhere that takes their fancy. A news photographer might travel to anywhere there is news. Some photographers and photographer's assistants find work shooting pictures for catalogs, Web sites, scientific journals, and research facilities. For instance, large clothing chains often maintain an image library of products.

Most photographer's assistants work in New York, Los Angeles, or other major cities. As the media and entertainment centers for the United States and the world, these are natural focus points for aspiring photographers. Sometimes the creative energy at a shoot and having to deal with so many demanding people can create a lot of stress. The ability to remain calm, polite, and effective in all situations is very important for photographer's assistants.

Hours can vary. While some jobs, such as shooting products for a catalog, may have a regular 9-to-5, 40-hour workweek, most do not. Like all artists, photographers can keep strange hours. Some shoots will take place during the day, some at night. Some photographers will work weekends, while some won't. Sometimes, shoots are limited by

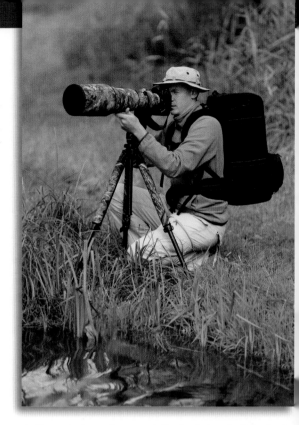

▲ Some photographers specialize in photos of wild animals. These professionals may have to work in extreme weather conditions and perhaps dangerous situations.

TALKING TRENDS

According to the Department of Labor, the number of photographers (and photographer's assistants) is expected to grow at a rate of about 3 percent through 2024. However, competition for these jobs is fierce. The large number of people entering the field will keep wages low and opportunities scarce for all but the most talented and in-demand photographers.

the subjects' or the studio's schedule. If a particular model, actor, or athlete is available only on Tuesday evenings, that is when you will have to work. You will need to be flexible and available whenever you are needed.

A photographer's assistant's job is not easy. Keeping track of everything and dealing with so many problems so the photographer can concentrate on his or her job is not for the faint of heart! Many feel, however, that the nature of the job makes up for these inconveniences. You will get to meet and interact with interesting and, occasionally, famous people and work with the latest and best photography equipment.

A Typical Day

Here are the highlights of a typical day for a photographer's assistant.

Lights! Today the photographer you work for will be shooting a fashion spread for a well-known magazine. Hours before the models arrive, though, you're on the set setting up the lights, loading the cameras, and making sure the food arrives.

Camera! The next 14 hours are a blur of work. As soon as one roll of film is shot, you reload the camera and hand it off. Another assistant takes the film, writes down what's on it, and safely stores it.

Action! After a long day, you're tired and want to go home. But there's still more to be done. The lights and equipment need to be broken down, and the studio needs to be closed up.

▲ In addition to loading and reloading cameras, you may need to change camera lenses too.

NOTES FROM THE FIELD

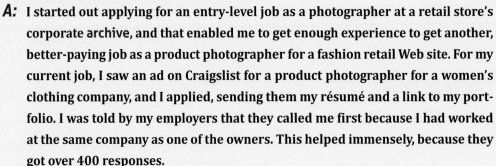

Photographer, Brooklyn, New York

Q: *How did you get your job?*

A: I started out applying for an entry-level job as a photographer at a retail store's corporate archive, and that enabled me to get enough experience to get another, better-paying job as a product photographer for a fashion retail Web site. For my current job, I saw an ad on Craigslist for a product photographer for a women's clothing company, and I applied, sending them my résumé and a link to my portfolio. I was told by my employers that they called me first because I had worked at the same company as one of the owners. This helped immensely, because they got over 400 responses.

Q: *What do you like best about your job?*

A: The freedom, physically and socially. I don't have to go to an office and sit behind a desk all day, which I love. I also don't have to participate in any corporate or office politics, which is also great. At my current job, because it's a new company, I also get to interact directly with the owners and have a lot of input about the Web site and marketing of their Web business.

Q: *What's the most challenging part of your job?*

A: Negotiating for things that I need—whether that be requesting more equipment to get the job done, or trying to come to an agreement about exactly what my job entails and how much money I will be paid for my work. A lot of people in business don't understand the amount of time, equipment, and money that goes into making good photographs.

Q: *What are the keys to success as a photographer?*

A: Having good communication skills, good organizational skills, and a good head for business. Of course, you need to be able to do the kind of work you're applying for or putting in a bid for, but being a good businessperson is equally, if not more important, in the big picture. Also, you have to be a patient person, and able to deal with lots of different kinds of people, some of whom are stressed out or overworked when they are calling you.

Start Preparing Now

- Learn all you can about photography. If you can, ask a professional photographer if you can observe a shoot, so that you know what goes on.

- Try to meet professional photographers. One handshake is worth any number of e-mails.

- Build a **portfolio** of your own work. Prospective employers will want some assurance that you know what you're doing. A Web site is an excellent place to display your work.

Training and How to Get It

The entire purpose of working as a photographer's assistant is to gain experience in photography. The job can, in many ways, be thought of as an apprenticeship. However, this does not mean that you should not seek to educate yourself. Before looking for a job as a photographer's assistant, it is important to know a lot about all sorts of cameras, both digital and film,

▲ Photographers will often edit photos so the image will appear brighter and crisper when reproduced. The photo on the left is unedited while the one the right has been digitally enhanced. Adobe Photoshop is the most-used digital editing software.

as well as photographic equipment. Working in a camera store can be valuable training, as can reading books on photography and subscribing to photographic magazines. A good understanding of art history and symbolism is also helpful.

Because of the increasing popularity of digital photography (even pictures taken on film are often scanned when used for professional production), you will need to be good with computers. The industry standard for retouching blemishes, adjusting colors and light, and many other applications is Adobe's Photoshop. Learn how to use this important computer program!

Attending trade and vocational schools, as well as community college courses, can help you learn the technical aspects of photography. There are also schools, such as the School of Visual Arts in New York City, that offer everything from evening courses to degrees in fine arts such as photography. However, you won't get as much "real world" experience in such places as you would working as an assistant and shooting your own pictures. Furthermore, you will not be making the contacts you need to further your career. For this reason, many working artists consider formal education in photography to be unnecessary.

For more on how to begin as a photographer's assistant, see "Finding a Job," below.

Learn the Lingo

Here are a few words you'll hear as a photographer's assistant:

- **Transparency** The professional name for a photographic "slide," as you would use in a slide projector. Slides generally have better color reproduction and last longer.

- **Back lighting** Placing the light source so the subject is between the camera and the light.

- **Light meter** A very useful device that tells you exactly how much light you have to work with. Because the human eye adjusts to light levels, it can be difficult to tell how what you see will look on film. The light meter accurately reads the light levels.

Finding a Job

Finding a job can be the hardest part of being a photographer's assistant. Occasionally newspapers or (more usually) sites such as Craigslist (http://www.craigslist.org) or Monster (http://www.monster.com) will have help-wanted ads. However, if you are going to succeed in photography, you are going to have to take matters into your own hands. Go out of your way to build a portfolio, attend gallery openings, meet professional photographers, and otherwise try to enter the world of professional photography.

The first and most important thing is that any inquiry to become a photographer's assistant should be accompanied by a thoroughly proofread and artistically well-designed résumé. Building a résumé can take time, and writing a résumé is an art in itself, but if done well, it will indicate not only that you are a hard worker but that you pay attention to detail and have an artist's eye. Indicating in your query letter or e-mail that you are available any time, day or night, can help, as many professional photographers keep erratic schedules.

Finally, network. Get to know professional photographers who might hire you. Many photographers prefer to work with people they already know. Social networking Web sites such as Instagram (www.instagram.com) and Flickr (www.flickr.com) are one way of doing this. Also check out sites that specialize in professional photographer portfolios, such as SmugMug (www.smugmug.com) and 500px (www.500px.com). Even better than social media, however, is attending photography events in person and introducing yourself. Additionally, create a Web site of your own to show your work to prospective clients and employers. Since many professionals already have assistants they work with regularly, offer to be an intern or second assistant, helping their helper. Again, the important thing is building relationships.

All of this takes a lot of time and pays very little money. You may need to take on a second or even third job in addition to working as a photographer's assistant, especially in expensive cities, such as New York, San Francisco, and Los Angeles. While you might want to start in a

See what it's like to be a travel photographer.

less expensive city, such as Chicago or Minneapolis, the best opportunities may be on the coasts—and remember, persistence is the key to success.

Tips for Success

- Photography, like all the arts, is a highly social profession. Being a "people person" is essential.

- Be organized! The photographer's assistant's real job is to be the one who knows where everything is and what happens next.

Reality Check

Photography is a very difficult industry to get ahead in. Photographer's assistants work long hours and are not paid very much. Very few can make ends meet by working in this industry alone.

LEARN MORE ONLINE

AMERICAN SOCIETY OF MEDIA PHOTOGRAPHERS (ASMP)
The ASMP is a top organization for professional photographers. http://www.asmp.org/

AMERICAN PHOTOGRAPHIC ARTISTS (APA)
Another key trade organization for professional photographers. http://www.apanational.com

Other Jobs to Think About

- Graphic designer. Like photographers, graphic designers must have a good "eye," but tend to work alone.

- TV/film camera operator. The skills needed for this job are much the same as for photography, but the work can be more steady.

- Photographic process workers. If you love photography, why not work in a developing studio? High-end professional camera stores require good, knowledgeable workers.

How to Move Up

- Sell your work. Most photographer's assistants are themselves photographers. The more you show your work to people, no matter if it's in an art gallery, a restaurant, or your living room, the more people will know your name.

- Sell yourself. If you have experience, make connections, get jobs, and sell your work!

- Sell out. Working in an office as a picture editor digitally retouching other people's photographs or shooting products for a catalog or Web site is not glamorous, but it does pay the bills.

TEXT-DEPENDENT QUESTIONS

1. *How many professional photographers are there in the United States?*

2. *What are some tasks an assistant might perform during a shoot? What about before or after it?*

3. *What is Photoshop?*

4. *What are some related jobs you might also consider?*

RESEARCH PROJECTS

1. *Work on your own photographic portfolio. You can use one of the paid sites mentioned above if you like, but you could also create a free Instagram account that's dedicated solely to your photography work. Keep seeking new and interesting places and people to photograph.*

2. *Look online to find professional photographers in your area and contact them to introduce yourself. Ask if they would let you watch them work.*

3. *Find out more about the group American Photographic Artists and consider joining at the student level. This will enable you to host your photography portfolio on their site and will also get you discounts to photography events in your area. More information can be found at http://apanational.org/join/entry/student-membership.*

Telecommunications Equipment Installer/ Repairer

4

Work for a large company. Visit a variety of job sites. Work outdoors and indoors.

WORDS TO UNDERSTAND

broadband: a method of transmission that is capable of sending large amounts of data quickly.

deregulation: the removal of government control or restrictions on business activity.

infrastructure: the physical elements that make up a system (for example, roads and bridges are part of the traffic infrastructure).

interface: the point where two systems connect.

router: a device that sends (or "routes") data where it needs to go along a network.

Though telephone systems have been around for more than a century and cable television since the late 1960s, the enormous growth of the Internet in the 1990s led to a demand for new communication **infrastructure**. Old-fashioned dial-up Internet access was simply too slow for the new wealth of sound, pictures, and video. Some way had to be found to connect schools, homes, and businesses for the high-speed transmission of data. The answer was to use the already existing cable and phone lines to provide **broadband** access. Telecommunications jobs were suddenly in

◄ A crew leader installs cellular antennas.

high demand, and installers found themselves connecting not just televisions but also computers. There are about 83.6 million broadband Internet users and 218,600 telecommunications equipment installers in the United States today.

Is This Job Right for You?

To find out if being a telecommunications equipment installer/repairer is right for you, read each of the following questions and answer "Yes" or "No."

Yes	No	1.	*Can you follow directions precisely?*
Yes	No	2.	*Do you work well independently?*
Yes	No	3.	*Do you always play by the rules?*
Yes	No	4.	*Are you good with tools?*
Yes	No	5.	*Are you good at math and science?*
Yes	No	6.	*Are you good with computers?*
Yes	No	7.	*Do you have good communications skills?*
Yes	No	8.	*Do you have a driver's license?*
Yes	No	9.	*Can you see in color?*
Yes	No	10.	*Are you in good physical shape?*

If you answered "Yes" to most of these questions, you might want to consider a career as a telecommunications equipment installer/repairer. To find out more about these jobs, read on.

What's the Work Like?

As their job title implies, phone and cable installers connect, repair, and maintain telecommunications lines to homes, schools, and businesses. Doing this, however, is not as easy as it sounds. Because cable and phone companies have many customers, they tightly schedule appointments to connect services. It is important to do your job quickly and well, because people may have to take time away from work or school in order to let you into their house.

When arriving on a job site, you must first locate the **interface** between the customer's property and the main cable. This is the cable that runs underground or on utility poles back to the distribution center. For landline telephone service, this will be a wall jack; for cable, this will be a coaxial cable. If no connection exists, you may have to create one. Some homes use

▲ Homes and small businesses depend on wireless routers and professionals to fix them for their Internet service.

satellite dishes instead of cable for their connections, while other people use wireless Internet, which may require you to set up a **router**.

The next task is to connect the home or business to the network, which may require joining, or splicing, cables. If wires need to be run through a living or work space, you will need to run them carefully so that they are out of the way. An authorization code must often be called in to the main office to start the "flow" of data. Then you must make sure that the telephone or cable box is properly connected to the system, and the box, in turn, is connected to the computer or television. Computers must often have the proper software and settings installed. Finally, you must test the system, explain to the customer how to use it, and then speed off to the next appointment.

Who's Hiring?

- Phone companies

- Cable companies

- Building equipment carriers

Where Are the Jobs?

Because utilities such as telephone and cable can cause a lot of disruption when the main lines are laid through city streets, governments grant limited monopolies to the companies who own these systems. Many phone and cable installers, therefore, work for these big companies. But as **deregulation** has changed the industry, increasing numbers of private companies are getting in

TALKING MONEY

The median income for phone and cable installers is $53,640 per year, but can vary between $30,370 and $79,500. Those working for wired telecommunications carriers, such as phone and cable companies, tend to make the most, and those working in utility construction, who install new lines, tend to make the least.

▲ Aboveground main lines mean that workers must climb utility poles to repair problems up high.

on the telecommunications game. Other installers and repairers work for construction contractors and other companies who have an interest in wiring buildings.

The places where you may install phone or cable lines are as varied as the homes, businesses, and schools that need high-speed, modern communications. Within these places, you may also need to climb ladders, go up on roofs and balconies, or access other hard-to-reach places where cables need to be spliced. You will sometimes have to lift heavy bales of cable or toolboxes.

Working as a telecommunications equipment installer/repairer can be very hectic. You may have to deal with many customers in one day, and have little time to do each job. You may also have to deal with people who blame you for things that aren't your fault, such as utility outages. However, many people see dealing with many different people and not having to work in an office as one benefit of this job.

A Typical Day

Here are the highlights of a typical day for a cable installer.

Getting there is half the fun. Today you will be installing a cable modem for a new tenant in a Manhattan apartment building. The first challenge, of course, is finding the address.

Dealing with the customers. You find the building with little problem, but the customer is angry that you weren't there an hour ago. After she locks her overly friendly dog up in the bedroom, you get to work connecting the system to the main line—which, it turns out, means going up the fire escape to the roof of the building.

Testing it out. The tester says that the line is functioning, but her computer still can't get on the Internet. After you adjust a few settings, everything is working fine. On to the next job!

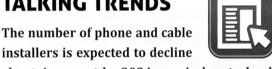

TALKING TRENDS

The number of phone and cable installers is expected to decline about 4 percent by 2024, as wireless technology makes much of the old system obsolete and people give up their landlines in increasing numbers. That said, people with strong customer service skills will always be needed in the telecommunications industry.

Start Preparing Now

- Learn how phone and cable systems work, and how computers connect to the Internet.

- Learn about electronics. A phone or cable system is much like an electrical circuit.

- Pay attention in math and science classes. These teach the principles by which phone and cable systems work.

Training and How to Get It

Most phone and cable installers are trained by the companies they work for. You may have to serve apprenticeships lasting one to three years. You may also have to attend training given by equipment suppliers or other companies. Some certification programs are offered

◀ An apprentice repairs cable lines in a customer's home.

through unions and other organizations. For instance, the Society of Cable Television Engineers has a certification program for cable installers and repairers offered through local SCTE chapters.

There are also trade and technical programs, lasting one year or more, that are often offered by local community colleges and trade and vocational schools in cooperation with utility companies. Such courses will teach you about electricity, electronics, communications technology. Many are hands-on, offering practical experience as well. Meanwhile, pay attention in high school. Math, science, and computer courses all teach you the essential skills you will need later.

Some important assets are a driver's license, color vision, and mechanical ability. Because you will need to get from job site to job site, it is essential to be able to drive. Because many wires and cables are color coded, color-blind people can have difficulty distinguishing between them. Because you will need to connect, separate, and splice cables, it is important to be good with tools.

Check out this video about telecommunications training.

Learn the Lingo

Here are a few words you'll hear as a telecommunications equipment installer/repairer:

- **DSL** Digital subscriber line—high-speed Internet access through a phone line.

- **Coaxial cable** An electrical cable surrounded by an insulator, used to carry a high-frequency signal.

- **IP** Internet protocol, a unique numerical address that lets computers talk to one another over the Internet.

Finding a Job

Look online for job listings in the telecommunications field. Phone and cable companies often advertise for installers in local newspapers and on their Web sites. You might also research the companies in your area and call or e-mail to ask about job opportunities

NOTES FROM THE FIELD

Cable installer, Jacksonville, Florida

Q: *How did you get your job?*

A: Nine years ago, I did what people used to do—look at the want ads in the paper. Two months after I sent my résumé (and had practically forgotten about it), I had my first interview. A month later, I was in the cable television industry.

Q: *What do you like best about your job?*

A: I am challenged daily to explain technical things to nontechnical people. In many cases, you have to figure out how to get a person to understand what you are saying and then deliver instructions to them so that they can understand and retain it. I love the look a person gets when they "get" what I am explaining to them.

Q: *What's the most challenging part of your job?*

A: I find it difficult to check and make sure that every channel, every computer, and every phone is working 100 percent correctly. This seems like it would be easy to do, but when you are dealing with four TVs, three computers, and five phones, it can be difficult. Not to mention the wiring, the education of the customer, and the little challenges that go with adding tons of wiring to a house. For example, crawling through an attic on a hot day and going under a house after a heavy rain.

Q: *What are the keys to success as a cable installer?*

A: In my job, it is critical to fix it right the first time. When we have to go to a job again and again, it wastes my company's money and steals important time away from the customer. Paying attention to detail, even for difficult service calls and installations, is very important. You have to be flexible. You can't take five hours to do a job that statistics show usually takes 30 minutes. Finally, you must keep everything you work with organized. I work out of a van, and if things get out of place, it takes me time to hunt them down. It's fairly easy to let it go and let it get dirty, but it really hurts you when you need to find that one piece of equipment.

▲ A telephone repair technician fixes a cable line.

and training programs. Generally, the department you will want to speak to is Human Resources. The company may give you further tips for what qualifications they look for in applicants.

You may also want to ask local trade and vocational schools about their training programs. Such schools often have placement programs with local utility companies.

Tips for Success

• Always be polite and friendly to the customer. A positive attitude is infectious.

• Take the time to do the job right. There's no going back on a tight schedule.

Reality Check

Phone and cable installers often have tight schedules and high workloads. They are also dependent on one company for their jobs. Finally, the telecommunications field is changing rapidly and some skills could be obsolete in a few years, so look for ways to learn new skills that will keep you in demand once you embark on your career.

Related Jobs to Consider

Electrician. Electricians also deal with wires and cables but are skilled laborers who make good salaries.

Line installer and repairer. These workers install and repair high-voltage cables. This job can be dangerous, but pays very well.

Computer network technician. Help to maintain and expand computer networks.

LEARN MORE ONLINE

SCTE
The Society of Cable Telecommunications Engineers, offering training and advocacy. http://www.scte.org/international.cfm

HOW TELEPHONES WORK
An explanation from Explain That Stuff! http://www.explainthatstuff.com/telephone.html

How to Move Up

- Become a manager. In time, you may be able to supervise other cable or phone installers.

- Get additional training. The more you know, the more jobs will open up to you, such as maintaining the main lines that run to the central offices—a responsibility that offers steady and well-paying work.

- Go back to school. More advanced managerial positions generally require a college degree.

TEXT-DEPENDENT QUESTIONS

1. *What are some of the tasks a telecommunications installer would expect to do?*

2. *What is the median salary of a phone/cable installer?*

3. *What are some of the qualities that make someone good at this job?*

4. *How might you start looking for a job in this field?*

RESEARCH PROJECTS

1. *Look online to create a list of different telecommunications companies in your area; some will be large multinational corporations like AT&T while others will be smaller, locally owned businesses. Find out if they are hiring or if they offer training programs for recent graduates.*

2. *Get to know the telecommunications set-up in your own home. What equipment and services does your family use? How is it arranged? Is the wi-fi reception better in one part of your home than in another? Do some research to see if there is anything you could do to make your home system work better.*

▲ In areas not wired for cable, a telecommunications installer may need to install a satellite antenna.

Computer Support Specialist

5

Be a problem solver. Work in the fast-paced world of computers. Be part of a team.

WORDS TO UNDERSTAND

carpal tunnel syndrome: a condition that causes intense pain in the nerves of the hand; usually caused by repetitive motions, such as using a keyboard.

domestic: here, the opposite of foreign; something within the United States.

offshoring: the practice of moving business tasks to foreign countries where people speak English but wages are much lower.

The call comes in from a panicked office worker: She has to make a presentation in half an hour and she just lost the file she was working on. Is there anything you can do? Fortunately, you are able to diagnose the problem and help her recover her work in the nick of time—just another day in the life of a computer support specialist. If you have a knack for technology, good people skills, and a talent for solving problems, this may be the career for you. With companies small and large relying more and more on computers, computer support specialists are critical to the running of modern businesses. Today there are nearly 767,000 computer support specialists working everywhere in America, from high-powered law firms in the office towers of Manhattan to call centers maintained by software companies in rural areas.

◀ Being a computer support specialist takes a knack for technology, patience, and a talent for solving problems.

Is This Job Right for You?

To find out if being a computer support specialist is right for you, read each of the following questions and answer "Yes" or "No."

Yes	*No*	**1.**	*Are you a good problem solver?*
Yes	*No*	**2.**	*Do you stay calm in high-stress situations?*
Yes	*No*	**3.**	*Do people often ask you for help with their computers?*
Yes	*No*	**4.**	*Are you patient?*
Yes	*No*	**5.**	*Do you have good written and spoken communications skills?*
Yes	*No*	**6.**	*Do you like to work indoors in an office environment?*
Yes	*No*	**7.**	*Are you good at both giving and following directions?*
Yes	*No*	**8.**	*Can you work as part of a team?*
Yes	*No*	**9.**	*Are you polite and respectful?*
Yes	*No*	**10.**	*Do you like helping people?*

If you answered "Yes" to most of these questions, you might want to consider a career as a computer support specialist. To find out more about this job, read on.

What's the Work Like?

Computer support specialists generally deal with three types of computer problems: hardware, software, or systems such as computer networks that enable computers to talk to one another. Some computer support specialists deal with all three types of issues, while others focus on a single issue, such as supporting a specific software program or hardware component.

Computer support specialists receive communications from users by e-mail or by phone. Often the customers are anxious or upset. A lot of money—or even their jobs—might be riding on the data in their computers. Other times, the people you are helping have just bought your company's hardware or software product and

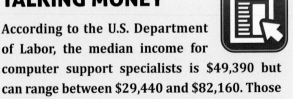

TALKING MONEY

According to the U.S. Department of Labor, the median income for computer support specialists is $49,390 but can range between $29,440 and $82,160. Those working for computer software publishers assisting customers tend to make the most, and those working in schools and universities the least.

▲ Computer support specialists are able to communicate with their users via e-mail or telephone. Sometimes, they can remotely access your computer to solve a problem.

think that it isn't working properly. Sometimes customers simply don't know how to use their computers properly.

Your job is to diagnose and fix their problems, if possible. If the problem is too complicated, or if you cannot understand what has gone wrong, you may have to refer the user to a specialist with more experience. You will then record the problem and give the user a ticket number. The problem will then be placed in a queue, or list, to be fixed by a second-level member of the support team. These support tracking systems make it easier to manage problems and see what

TALKING TRENDS

Because of the ever-increasing importance of computers in our lives, the number of computer support specialists will grow by about 12 percent through 2024 according to the U.S. Department of Labor. The practice of offshoring may mean fewer jobs in the United States and Canada. That said, a noticeable number of firms are bucking the offshoring trend, even basing publicity campaigns around the fact that they hire domestic support teams.

▲ It's important to provide users with the most up-to-date information security. If a data breach is detected, the issue will need to be resolved swiftly and efficiently.

the most common problems are. The tracking system can also help to control workers' time. In such systems, a support specialist may be scheduled to spend a certain amount of time out of every workday tracking problems and a certain amount of time fixing them. Computer and software companies value computer support specialists. Since they are the first to receive customers' complaints about hardware and software, they can provide valuable information on how to improve a product. They can also suggest ways in which products can be made easier to use, and give feedback on what most confuses customers.

A vital role played by more and more computer support teams is *information security*, or helping users keep their data secure from hackers and computer viruses. In addition to staying on top of some fairly complex technical issues, information security also involves educating users about the important role they themselves have to play in keeping networks safe.

Who's Hiring?

- Software publishers

- Private businesses of all kinds

- Religious and not-for-profit foundations

- Government agencies

- Public and private schools, kindergarten through 12th grade

- Colleges and universities

Where Are the Jobs?

Computer support specialists usually work in comfortable, well-lit offices and computer labs. The job sites tend to be a little chilly, since computer equipment requires air-conditioning to keep from overheating. The job tends to involve sitting at a desk, with little moving about. However, some lifting, such as moving and installing new computers, may also be required. Like all workers who use computers for long periods of time, computer support specialists may risk eyestrain, back problems, and joint problems, such as **carpal tunnel syndrome**. Because companies may have customers all over the world in different time zones or

▲ Although much of this job requires tech support via phone or e-mail, there is a chance that you will have to install new computers too.

employees who work odd hours, computer support specialists may have to work night or weekend shifts.

The size of a computer support specialist's office may have no relation to the size of the organization. A university may have only a few support specialists on call for hundreds or thousands of users, while a relatively small software company may maintain a center staffed with hundreds of employees in order to handle the traffic from thousands or millions of customers. The computer support specialist's day varies widely. You may be more or less busy, waiting for calls or e-mails to come in, or handling one problem after another with very little downtime.

A Typical Day

Here are the highlights of a typical day for a computer support specialist at a large company.

Field some calls. The day starts getting busy around 9:30 or 10 a.m., when users begin starting up their computers and running into trouble with their work. Some calls will be serious, such as hard-disk crashes that ruin hours of hard work. Some will seem silly, such as the boss who can't read his e-mail since his secretary, who usually prints it out for him, is on vacation. Other things will be routine administrative tasks, such as setting up usernames and passwords for new employees.

Handle an emergency. Suddenly, the call board lights up. The server on which the company's employees save their work has crashed. Dozens of users can't get to their important documents. While the network team tries to get it running again, you spend your time on the phone reassuring anxious employees.

See a typical day in the life of a computer support specialist.

Pull some overtime. The network team gets the server up and running again, but because of the disruption to the workday you need to stay late. In this case, you spend an extra hour answering users' e-mails from the previous day that you couldn't get to because of the network outage.

Start Preparing Now

- Learn as much as you can. Potential employers will want to know that you know your way around computers.

- Practice your written and oral communications skills. A computer support specialist must be polite, professional, and articulate.

- See if you can enroll in a training course to obtain certification in specialized software or hardware.

- While using your computer, practice describing your actions with words.

▲ Have a broken computer lying around? Brush up on your skills and work on fixing the machine.

NOTES FROM THE FIELD

Computer support specialist, *Kalamazoo, Michigan*

Q: *How did you get your job?*

A: It began as a work/study job. Later I got a call from my former supervisor asking me to fill a temporary position while they completed a job search. When the search was up they asked me if I'd stay on in another position doing hardware, software, printer, network, phone, Web, and e-mail tech support over the phone. I accepted!

Q: *What do you like best about your job?*

A: Getting to work with and provide help to a wide variety of people.

Q: *What's the most challenging part of your job?*

A: Learning to manage my reactions to customers' frequently emotional calls. People generally don't call the help desk to say they're happy and that everything is working perfectly for them.

Q: *What are the keys to success as a computer support specialist?*

A: Remember the Golden Rule. Wonderful people sometimes make stupid mistakes, but they still deserve to be treated like wonderful people. Don't let customers' frustration bring you down. Refocus yourself before each call and give each caller the benefit of your best effort. You don't have to be cheerful every minute of every day, but you'll go further if people think you are.

Learn the Lingo

Here are a few words you'll hear as a computer support specialist:

- **Server** A central computer that provides services to other computers. It can also act as storage space for data.

- **Network** Many computers linked together by servers. Networks can make it easier to share and store data but can create a lot of trouble when they break.

- **LBT** (local bug tracker). This is the "queue" into which users' errors are entered and trends recorded. LBTs are very important for tracking problems until they are resolved.

Training You'll Need

Though a college degree is not always necessary to work at a help desk, you will likely be competing for jobs with people who have had some college experience. Any advantage you can get, such as a practical familiarity with computers, will help you to get ahead. Since computer systems can be slightly different, computer support specialists will usually also be trained by the companies that employ them. This will usually include familiarization with the various computer programs used by the help desk and the process by which problems are resolved. Later you might be taught how to fix certain malfunctions, such as server crashes. Computer support specialists enjoy great upward mobility and are promoted based on their success at helping customers. As computer support specialists move up in the ranks, they are given more responsibilities, including performing second-level support. Learning how to perform these tasks is often accomplished more by experience than by formal training. At the top levels, they may help guide a company's overall use of computer technology. If further training is required, such as learning how to fix or run certain software, your company may pay for you to take a certification exam.

Finding a Job

Companies often place help-wanted ads in newspapers or online job-search sites such as Monster (www.monster.com). Also consider asking friends and relatives who work in technical support. They may be aware of entry-level openings at their companies or one with which they work. Computer support specialists are in great demand in all sorts of industries, from agribusiness to zoological parks. While computer support specialists are in demand in cities with large high-tech companies, such as New York, San Francisco Bay area (home of Apple, Facebook, Google, and many others), and Seattle (home of Amazon and Microsoft), modern telecommunications mean that call centers can also be located in rural areas. Show your work ethic, communications skills, and level-headed but friendly personality, both in your interview and by asking adults who write character references and letters of recommendation for you to emphasize these qualities. Make sure your résumé includes all the computer-related jobs that you have had and all the computer skills you possess. If you are looking for experience, consider an unpaid internship or even volunteering as a moderator on an Internet message board.

Tips for Success

- Be polite and calm. Resist the urge to make fun of users. Many older people see computers as new and scary, and may be afraid of breaking them.

- Get your certification as soon as possible. It's your ticket to moving up.

Reality Check

Many call centers are dead-end jobs, with little opportunity to move up. Furthermore, screening the same call over and over again can be very tedious. Finally, many users can be rude or downright hostile.

LEARN MORE ONLINE

HELP DESK MANAGEMENT COMMUNITY PORTAL
Learn what a help desk is, and what it does, and make contact with industry professionals. http://www.helpdesking.com

TREND MICRO
Check out the Web site of a massive computer support company that offers a wide variety of different products and services to assist individuals and companies with their technology needs. http://www.trendmicro.com

Related Jobs to Consider

Computer programmer. Many computer programmers are self-taught. If you are a skilled programmer, you can get a well-paying job making programs or games. If you are right for help desk work, you may be a few courses and an interview away from being a programmer.

Network administrator. Computer network administrators are in charge of building and maintaining companies' computer networks. Though this job often requires advanced certification, such certification may only require some light coursework.

Quality-assurance specialist. If you don't like dealing with people, but do like tinkering with computers, you might like to work as a quality-assurance (QA) specialist. QA is the department in charge of making sure software works as advertised.

How to Move Up

- Get certified. Some companies, such as Microsoft, have special training courses that teach people how to fix their products. By earning your certification, you can move up to a better-paying job as a network administrator

- Keep learning. Did you know many two- and four-year colleges give credit for work experience? You may find your local institution has favorable financial aid policies for working students. Many employers like to see a two- or four-year degree for higher-level employees, or even that you're working toward one. If you are working for a college or university, you can usually get free or reduced-cost tuition while you work.

- Be persistent. The help desk is usually the first step toward becoming a computer support specialist. Because the computer industry is changing so rapidly, formal training is of limited use. Many computer support specialists learn enough "on the job" to move up.

TEXT-DEPENDENT QUESTIONS

1. *What are a few of the most important jobs of a computer support specialist?*

2. *What personality traits might make someone successful at this job?*

3. *What sort of training is needed?*

RESEARCH PROJECTS

1. *Do you already feel pretty comfortable with computers? Test your support-giving skill by helping an older person with his or her devices. Afterwards, reflect on the experience: did you enjoy helping out, or did it make you feel stressed when the person didn't understand right away?*

2. *Check out this list of free online classes in computer support and sign up for one that makes sense for your current skill level: http://study.com/articles/10_Sources_for_Free_Online_Technology_Courses.html*

AutoCAD Technician, Graphic Production Technician

6

Learn the latest computer technology. Enter an exciting and fast-growing field. Work with high technology.

WORDS TO UNDERSTAND

aesthetic: refers to visual appearance, beauty, or design.

drafter: a person who creates (or "drafts") technical drawings that show how to construct a particular design.

lay out: to arrange elements in a deliberate way.

Computers have opened up many opportunities for people with visually oriented skills. Today everything from planning office buildings to creating books and magazines to printing vacation photographs is handled by computers and software. Chief among the software is a drafting program called AutoCAD (for computer-aided design), which is published by Autodesk. AutoCAD technicians use their software to design and **lay out** objects in three-dimensional space. Other kinds of software are used to produce everything from postage stamps to books to large highway billboards.

◀ Programs like AutoCAD are widely used in industries such as architecture and engineering.

Is This Job Right for You?

To find out if being an AutoCAD technician or graphic production technician is right for you, read each of the following questions and answer "Yes" or "No."

Yes	No	1. *Are you good with computers?*
Yes	No	2. *Do you have a keen sense of color and design?*
Yes	No	3. *Do you know how to follow directions?*
Yes	No	4. *Can you manage your time wisely?*
Yes	No	5. *Do you like working as part of a team?*
Yes	No	6. *Do you plan your work carefully?*
Yes	No	7. *Are you methodical and patient in your work?*
Yes	No	8. *Do you have a good sense of space?*
Yes	No	9. *Do you enjoy creative work?*
Yes	No	10. *Can you manage many tasks simultaneously?*

If you answered "Yes" to most of these questions, you might want to consider a career as an AutoCAD technician or graphic production technician. To find out more about these jobs, read on.

Who's Hiring?

- Architecture and interior design firms

- Universities and scientific firms

- Manufacturers

- Publishers

- Software companies

This video provides some basic information about what drafters do.

What's the Work Like?

AutoCAD technicians use Autodesk's AutoCAD program to produce three-dimensional representations of building interiors, furniture, landscapes, mechanical parts, or other objects.

AutoCAD uses simple objects, such as lines, circles, and arcs, to build more complex pictures of proposed projects. These help designers and engineers visualize how a project will work in real space.

Graphic production technician is a career choice that includes a wide range of job descriptions. A graphic production technician may do anything from making and printing signs and advertisements to designing complex visual animations for a video game or training program. These may be designed by the technician herself or by a professional graphic designer. Some of the software used includes Adobe's Illustrator and Photoshop, which are graphics software, and Adobe's InDesign, a text layout and design program. The graphic production technicians may operate complicated printers and other machinery.

▲ Designers may use software programs to draft projects such as a new car design.

Where Are the Jobs?

Most AutoCAD technicians and graphic production technicians work in comfortable, well-lit, climate-controlled offices. The offices tend to be a little chilly, since computer equipment requires air-conditioning to keep from overheating. The job tends to involve sitting at a desk, with little moving about. However, like all workers who use computers for long periods of time, people who use AutoCAD may risk eyestrain, back problems, and joint problems, such as carpal tunnel syndrome. They usually work 40-hour weeks but may need to put in overtime on projects with impending deadlines.

A Typical Day

Here are the highlights of a typical day for an AutoCAD technician.

Get the plan. Your architecture firm has been hired to redesign the interior of a country club. Today you'll need to input the architect's plans into AutoCAD to see how the designs translate from 2-D to 3-D.

Meet with the client. The architect presents your renderings to the client that very afternoon. They are impressed with the plans but offer some suggestions.

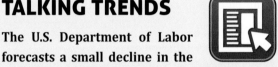

TALKING TRENDS

The U.S. Department of Labor forecasts a small decline in the need for AutoCAD technicians by 2024, simply because, as the technology improves and the process of drafting becomes increasingly automated, fewer workers may be needed. That said, as technology becomes increasingly central to all types of graphic design, skilled technicians are likely to always be in demand.

Burn the midnight oil. Long after everyone else has left for the night, you're still hard at work, correcting the plans to correspond to the client's wishes.

Start Preparing Now

- Learn all you can about AutoCAD and digital imaging software.

- Pay attention in school. Mathematics and physics are especially important, and English classes will help you to fluently communicate your designs and ideas.

- Potential employers will want to know that you are proficient in the software. Develop a portfolio of designs and other work to show them.

▲ Images like these can be part of a presentation by an architecture firm at a meeting, with a client. If the client is not satisfied, it's back to the drawing board.

Training and How to Get It

Because there are many types of jobs for AutoCAD technicians and graphic production technicians, there are many ways to approach this work. Most importantly, you will need to be familiar with the relevant software and hardware. This usually includes computers (particularly those made by Apple, a company that has long dominated the graphic design field), programs such as Adobe's Photoshop, and, of course, Autodesk's AutoCAD. Sometimes you can teach yourself how to use these tools of the trade. It is also possible to take courses at a community college or trade school. Some training may be available on the job. Because many of the software programs and much of the equipment can be expensive, it is hard for private individuals or even high schools to acquire the necessary tools.

Many jobs in graphic design require a college education. However, it's also possible to work your way up from the bottom. If you are skilled at what you do, the sky's the limit.

Learn the Lingo

Here are a few words you'll hear as an AutoCAD technician, graphic production technician, or digital imaging technician:

- **AutoCAD** Autodesk's commonly used two- and three-dimensional design program.

- **Photoshop** Published by Adobe Systems, this is the industry standard photo-manipulation software. "Photoshop" is also commonly used as a verb for manipulating a picture.

- **InDesign** Published by Adobe Systems, InDesign is a powerful program that enables a user to design and lay out a publication.

◀ Translating real life into three-dimensional schematics is the challenge for an AutoCAD technician.

NOTES FROM THE FIELD

AutoCAD technician, New York, New York

Q: *How did you get your job?*

A: It was all about timing. I was looking for a job at the time and walked by this really beautiful furniture showroom in Manhattan. I just randomly asked one of the salespeople if there were any design positions available. They said their AutoCAD technician had just left and they were looking for another, so I sent them my résumé and, after three interviews, I scored the job as an interior designer/AutoCAD tech.

Q: *What do you like best about your job?*

A: Well. I love using AutoCAD, and I get to use it a lot each day working on fun projects of all kinds and sizes, which has helped me improve my CAD skills tremendously.

Q: *What's the most challenging part of your job?*

A: Since it is a furniture showroom, you have to constantly be on your toes and produce floor plans and other drawings quickly and accurately for clients who are constantly coming in, whether by appointment or not. I make all the AutoCAD drawings in the showroom for six salespeople with dozens and dozens of regular and new clients. I also have other responsibilities in the office, so I'm multitasking all day long.

Q: *What are the keys to success as an AutoCAD technician?*

A: I'd say, like for any job, you have to have good time-management skills, patience, a good attitude, and the ability to learn quickly and the desire to learn more. I think most importantly, you can't take the job too seriously. It's just a job—it shouldn't run your life. There has to be a balance.

Finding a Job

Openings for AutoCAD technicians and graphic production technicians are often posted online or published in newspapers. Most are with large companies. Also look at online job-search sites such as Monster (http://www.monster.com). You may also want to send your résumé to architecture firms, print shops, and other businesses if they have any openings. While workers such as these are especially in demand in cities with large publishing industries and high-tech companies, there are opportunities all over the country. Make sure your résumé includes all the computer-related jobs that you have had. If you are looking for experience, consider an unpaid internship or even volunteering for a church or community organization. Being able to show your skill with the requisite software is critical in securing employment.

LEARN MORE ONLINE

AUTODESK
Publishers of AutoCAD. http://www.autodesk.com

THE HITCHHIKER'S GUIDE TO AUTOCAD BASICS
A user-friendly introduction to the software. http://autode.sk/2xfwsr3

Tips for Success

- Keep abreast of the latest technical developments. The technology used in these jobs often changes rapidly. One way to do this is by reading trade magazines and specialist Web sites.

- Develop your sense of design. Also, it's never too early to learn how to use the required software.

Reality Check

Many AutoCAD technicians and graphic production technicians. Though work experience counts for much in this field, be aware that you will be competing with college graduates for jobs.

Related Jobs to Consider

Photographer. Photographers must also have a keen **aesthetic** sense, but the work is much less technical.

Prepress technician. Prepress technicians work in the same industries and do similar digital imaging work.

Desktop publisher. Design and lay out printed materials.

How to Move Up

- Improve your software skills. The more you learn, the more valuable you are to your employer.

- Go back to school. Education often helps workers land more responsible and lucrative jobs.

TEXT-DEPENDENT QUESTIONS

1. *What fields often use AutoCAD?*

2. *Beyond AutoCAD, what are some of the other types of software that graphic production technicians use?*

3. *What can you do right now to help improve your job prospects in this field?*

4. *What's a prepress technician?*

RESEARCH PROJECTS

1. *Check out AutoDesk's online learning pages (http://au.autodesk.com/au-online/overview) and get to know the software a little bit. You might even download a free trial (https://www.autodesk.com/products/autocad/free-trial) that you can experiment with. Consider if this is something you would want to work with day in and day out.*

2. *Search for "graphical production technician" jobs on a career site such as Monster (www.monster.com). What are the requirements? Do these jobs sound like something you would enjoy? If you can find any jobs in your immediate area, consider contacting the company for more information about what they do.*

Set Decorator, Props Person

7

Help to make props and sets for TV and movies. Exercise your creativity. Work in an exciting and creative industry.

WORDS TO UNDERSTAND

armorer: person in charge of weapons on a film or TV set; also called weapons master.

internship: a low-level assistant or trainee job, usually taken to gain experience.

irregular: unpredictable.

Who do you think gets the most work in the TV and motion picture industries? Actors? Directors? No—it's the art department. The art department is the single largest department on a movie set. It is responsible for creating the "look" of the film and includes such elements as design, construction, props, special effects, costumes, and others. Job titles include painters, riggers, sculptors, prop makers, model makers, stagehands, and special effects, and may even be considered to include animal handlers and **armorers**. It is hard to say how many people work in these capacities in the U.S. film industry, but according to the U.S. Department of Labor, about 12,000 people work in arts and entertainment as set and exhibit designers or as artists and related professionals. Set decorators and props people work in music, theater, and stage productions too.

◀ **Have you ever wondered why some castles look incredibly realistic in movies? Although some are generated by computer, others, like this model of the Hogwarts castle in the Harry Potter movies, are built by hand and inserted into the picture.**

Is This Job Right for You?

To find out if working in an art department is right for you, read each of the following questions and answer "Yes" or "No."

Yes	*No*	**1.** *Do you love making things?*
Yes	*No*	**2.** *Are you willing to work long or irregular hours?*
Yes	*No*	**3.** *Can you improvise well?*
Yes	*No*	**4.** *Are you very organized?*
Yes	*No*	**5.** *Are you strong and in good shape?*
Yes	*No*	**6.** *Are you very creative?*
Yes	*No*	**7.** *Do you work well under pressure?*
Yes	*No*	**8.** *Are you willing to start at the bottom?*
Yes	*No*	**9.** *Are you a team player?*
Yes	*No*	**10.** *Do you have good communications skills?*

If you answered "Yes" to most of these questions, you might want to consider a career as a set decorator or props person. To find out more about this job, read on.

What's the Work Like?

Many of the jobs in the art department, such as production designer, are senior positions that involve researching and planning the overall look of the production. Once the plan is in place, the craftspeople of the art department swing into action.

Set decorators and *set dressers* are two related jobs that involve turning the set designer's vision into reality. For example, preparation to shoot a scene inside a kitchen might involve painting the walls to be the desired color, purchasing or creating appliances that match the period of the film, and

TALKING MONEY

It is hard to estimate average earnings for these jobs, both because so much of the work is irregular and because of the wide variety of positions. The median annual income for all workers in arts and entertainment is $58,390. Workers with regular jobs, such as with long-running Broadway shows and Hollywood production companies, will tend to be paid according to their specialty, such as carpenters and electricians. Workers who are union members will be paid according to union rates, which are generally higher than nonunion rates.

▲ Whether you are watching a serious film about politics or a fun thriller, each scene has been carefully constructed by set decorators.

finding the correct style of the curtains. If you see a particular type of clock in the background of the shot, it's because the art department decided it should be there.

Meanwhile, *props people* purchase or make items that are used by the actors—anything from a stone axe for a caveman to a corsage for the prom queen. They may order their own materials, particularly if they are freelancers, or they may leave this to the buyers. They will usually also offer feedback to the design department on how a particular idea is working out.

TALKING TRENDS

It is hard to estimate growth in the number of people working in art departments. There may be less growth, due to many movies now being filmed overseas. There will also be a lot of competition for jobs in this highly desirable and interesting industry.

Special effects workers have many specialties. They may operate mechanical dinosaurs or radio-controlled airplanes or be responsible for the gory splatter-factor in a horror movie. These days, a great many special effects workers use computers to fill in other effects after shooting is finished. *Pyrotechnicians,* a subspecialty of special effects workers, may set up and detonate anything from large explosions to *squibs,* or small explosive charges. Other pyrotechnic devices, such as fireworks, are also their responsibility.

Carpenters, painters, and other skilled trades are also essential to the production of motion pictures and stage shows. They make and decorate sets and some props. How to train to be a carpenter is dealt with more fully in Careers in Demand for High School Graduates: *Construction and Trades.*

Other miscellaneous jobs in the art department include *property buyers,* who purchase needed props (or the components for the props), *armorers,* who keep track of all the weapons used on a film and make sure that the actors and crew know how to use them properly, and *animal handlers,* who train everything from rats and roaches to horses and elephants and ensure the safety of their charges.

Stagehands, and other workers who move or operate things instead of making them, are dealt with in the chapter of this book on grips, stagehands, and set-up workers.

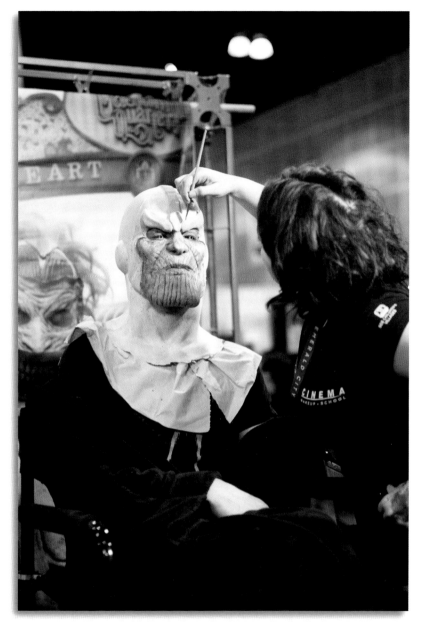

▲ Special effects in film can also include bringing to life freaky creatures like this one.

Who's Hiring?

- TV production companies

- Movie studios

- Local TV stations

- Commercial production companies

- Theaters and theater companies

- Musicians and touring companies

Where Are the Jobs?

Most openings are in Los Angeles or New York, since these cities both have large theater scenes and because many movies, television shows, and commercials are shot there. Set decorators and props people frequently work indoors in shops and production companies, but for filming on location, they may need to travel to distant parts of the country or the world.

Hours in the entertainment industry can be very **irregular**, with 14- to 18-hour days one month followed by long periods of unemployment. However, set decorators and props people in the motion picture industry tend to work for large craft houses and so have more regular jobs than many other workers. Also, if you are working for certain productions, such as a Broadway show, you might have a fairly regular work schedule.

Generally, the work is not particularly dangerous (with some exceptions, such as working with firearms or high explosives), but it can be stressful to work under pressure. Often you will have to complete one part of a movie's props while another is being shot.

A Typical Day

Here are the highlights of a typical day for someone working in an art department.

Planning stages. The first step before making anything is to find out what's expected of you. Today, for instance, you meet with the production designer and the director to find out how they want the inside of the spaceship *Lightning Bug* to look for their new film *Lightning Bug II: Cowboys in Space*. By the end of the meeting, you have a list of detailed instructions and sketches.

Send out the buyer. You compose a shopping list of what you'll need to construct the set. This is then given to the buyer, whose job it is to find all the various things for the job.

Make it! The cockpit of the *Lightning Bug* arrives at your workshop in the form of sheet metal, tubing, piping, and disassembled chairs from an office-supply store. By next week, though, you'll have this looking like a spaceship from the 26th century.

Start Preparing Now

- Work making props and special effects for student productions, independent movies, Web features, and anything else you can find. Do everything you can to gain experience.

- Study everything you can about how props and special effects for movies and TV shows are made. There are some trade magazines you can read.

Here is a video about the job of set decorator.

Training and How to Get It

Some set decorators and props people are self-trained or trained informally on the job. This is definitely an industry where you learn by doing and where experience counts. For this reason, it is best to get as much experience as possible to build up your résumé. Try to join community theater or independent movie productions. Many prop makers began by getting starter jobs or **internships** at production houses. The most important thing is to have a talent and a passion for what you're doing and not to mind working long hours.

Other jobs require a lot more training. Working with explosives or firearms, for instance, requires special permits and a lot of training. Many pyrotechnicians and armorers are former military or law-enforcement personnel. Carpenters often begin as carpenter's helpers and work their way up through experience. They may also attend technical or trade schools.

NOTES FROM THE FIELD

Metalworker, New York, New York

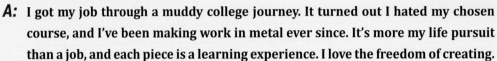

Q: *How did you get your job?*

A: I got my job through a muddy college journey. It turned out I hated my chosen course, and I've been making work in metal ever since. It's more my life pursuit than a job, and each piece is a learning experience. I love the freedom of creating.

Q: *What do you like best about your job?*

A: Most rewarding is the sense of creating something from nothing—there is an immense feeling of satisfaction at seeing something through, from concept to actual physical object, never mind that it attaches me to the lineage of metal-workers throughout all human history. I also cherish the effect my work has over people: Continuously, the public will stare, or start in on spontaneous conversation at the uniqueness, or otherwise striking quality, of my finished products.

Q: *What's the most challenging part of your job?*

A: Most challenging is making sure there are enough people tapped into my endeavors, so that I can feed myself and pay my bills. There is no clear "road to success" in my chosen field; it is a constant hustle. My lifestyle is not as stable as in other professions; I am continuously seeking new outlets so that my work may be further promoted and found valuable by others, so that they will share in my vision and help me continue making pieces that are compelling and powerful.

Q: *What are the keys to success?*

A: The keys to success are varied: It helps to be talented and possess a unique vision that shows in the making of each piece. Once original talent is taken care of, having a broad network of supporters or contacts is indispensable. This is a foundation for the promise of a bright future, as these people will be there to bounce ideas off of, help spread word about the specialness of your creativity, and serve as first (and repeat) clients for your distinctive, beautiful work. A job under someone experienced—in the same field—can provide valuable information not readily available. It is like an extension of an internship, or apprenticeship. Many gems of knowledge are passed along in this setting, especially if there is a good working relationship.

Learn the Lingo

There are a few different types of props:

- **Dressing prop** The furniture, carpets, and other decor used to decorate a set.

- **Hand prop** Any prop held by an actor, such as a laser gun or a riding crop.

- **Hero prop** A prop that is central to the action in a scene, such as an ancient artifact being grabbed by an intrepid archaeologist.

- **Stunt prop** A prop especially made to make stunts safer, such as a blunt, spring-loaded knife or a bottle made of "sugar glass."

- **Mechanical prop** A prop that moves or lights up.

Finding a Job

Production companies sometimes advertise in newspapers, free weeklies, and trade publications. Look also on Web sites such as Craigslist (http://www.craigslist.org) or Variety.com. Most handicraftspersons belong to unions, such as the International Alliance of Theatrical Stage Employees (IATSE). These unions are not easy to join, but they are very helpful for finding jobs for their members.

Tips for Success

- Pay attention to directions. Remember, your creation is supposed to contribute to the production as a whole.

- It is your reputation that gets you more work. Let the people in charge of productions know they can count on you.

Reality Check

Art departments are exciting, creative environments. However, the work can be irregular and sometimes stressful.

Related Jobs to Consider

Grip, stagehand, or set-up worker. Instead of making the scenery and props, why not move them around?

Camera operator. Camera operators are an important part of shooting any film or TV.

Computer animator. Computer animators are very important for adding special effects in postproduction.

LEARN MORE ONLINE

ARCHITECTURAL DIGEST: SET DESIGN
A collection of articles about the work going on behind the scenes of movie sets, fashion shows, and more. https://www.architectural-digest.com/celebrity-style/set-design

IATSE
The International Alliance of Theatrical Stage Employees, Moving Picture Technicians, Artists, and Allied Crafts—the union most craftspersons belong to. http://www.iatse-intl.org

How to Move Up

- Become a designer. Many stage designers started on the bottom, helping create other people's designs.

- Learn a trade. Skilled workers, such as carpenters and electricians, are indispensable to theatrical productions—and a lot better paid!

- Start your own company. If you become known for making model spaceships or stop-action dinosaurs, why not start a company specializing in that?

TEXT-DEPENDENT QUESTIONS

1. *What does a pyrotechnician do?*

2. *What sort of training is required to get jobs in this field?*

3. *What are some organizations that need to hire people in this field?*

4. *What is the primary union?*

RESEARCH PROJECTS

1. *Join your school drama club and volunteer to help with props and set construction. You could also offer to help at a local theater, if there is one in your community. Pay attention to how you feel about doing the job: is it satisfying?*

2. *Read some practical books about the field, such as* The Backstage Handbook *by Paul Carter,* Stagecraft Fundamentals *by Rita Kogler Carver, or* The Guerrilla Filmmakers Handbook *by Genevieve Jolliffe. As you read, try to picture yourself taking part in the activities described.*

▲ The person responsible for weapons on a film or TV set is called the armorer or weapons master.

Web Developer

8

Use sophisticated software. Work in an exciting hi-tech field. Exercise your creativity.

WORDS TO UNDERSTAND

back end: here, the software that makes computers and computer networks function that is not seen by users.

host: here, a company that provides technology and services to create and maintain Web sites.

offshoring: moving jobs to countries where labor is cheaper.

serve: here, to provide Web pages to other computers that request them.

stage presence: the ability to grab and hold an audience's attention.

Can anyone imagine life without the Internet? Beginning as a government project in the late 1960s, the Internet grew to enormous size in the mid-1990s after the invention of the World Wide Web. The Web lets us view text, pictures, sound, movies, and animation in an easy, user-friendly way. Finding driving directions, shopping for clothes, and looking up information are now only a few mouse clicks away. The people who make the magic happen are Web developers. Web developers write the computer code, design the graphics, and maintain the behind-the-scenes technology that keeps Web sites running. While not as fluent in computer code as the programmers who handle the **back end**, they work with clients to find out what they want and create sites that elegantly express what the clients have to say.

◀ A web developer often works remotely, communicating with clients via e-mail, phone, and Skype.

Is This Job Right for You?

To find out if being a Web developer is right for you, read each of the following questions and answer "Yes" or "No."

Yes	No	1.	*Are you good with computers?*
Yes	No	2.	*Are you familiar with the latest technology?*
Yes	No	3.	*Do you have a good sense of color and design?*
Yes	No	4.	*Do you keep at a problem until you solve it?*
Yes	No	5.	*Do you have a good work ethic?*
Yes	No	6.	*Do you listen carefully to others?*
Yes	No	7.	*Do you enjoy learning?*
Yes	No	8.	*Are you willing to work long hours?*
Yes	No	9.	*Are you always curious?*
Yes	No	10.	*Do you like to know what makes things work?*

If you answered "Yes" to most of these questions, then you might be cut out for a career as a Web page designer. To find out more about this job, read on.

What's the Work Like?

A Web site can be small and consist of only a few pages, or enormous and have sophisticated functions, such as message boards, e-commerce capability, and multimedia downloads. No matter what type of site it is, though, the "guts" of the World Wide Web is HTML, or *hypertext markup language*. HTML is a code that tells a browser how to display images and text on the screen. At the most basic level, a Web site is a number of HTML files linked together. The developer's job fundamentally consists of creating these files.

However, creating a Web site requires more than just writing HTML. A good Web developer knows how to do many other tasks. These include registering a domain

TALKING MONEY

The average annual income for Web developers is about $66,000. Those working in entry-level positions of computer support earn about $35,000 a year on average, according to figures from the U.S. Bureau of Labor Statistics. Salaries generally track with education and experience, but many in the field are self-taught or have learned their skills while working.

▲ All Web site development begins with the creation of HTML.

name (the address that appears in the navigation toolbar), and finding a **host** to **serve** the Web pages to users who request them. A Web developer will also know how to configure the server's setup and upload the Web site.

Some Web page designers use software such as Microsoft's Frontpage and Adobe's Dreamweaver to make Web pages. These *WYSIWYG* (for "what you see is what you get") programs make it easier to see what the finished Web page will look like. The most successful Web page designers know how to do far more than this, though. For instance, some know how to craft *PHP* (Personal Home Page tools) code to create dynamic Web sites that can

TALKING TRENDS

According to the U.S. Department of Labor, the number of Web developer jobs is expected to increase by as much as 27 percent by 2024. As more and more businesses depend on the Web to function, the need for developers is likely to grow. Opportunity may be slowed somewhat by offshoring, but frequently clients want to meet with the people who design and maintain their sites, which limits how much offshoring is possible.

▲ Each Web site is unique in its own way. Web developers must create sites specific to the needs of corporations, small businesses, or even bloggers.

quickly upload and change their content. Others are adept at creating applications, such as online shopping carts, in programming languages such as Java, or creating animations in Flash. The more you know how to do, the better your chances of succeeding as a Web page designer.

Who's Hiring?

- All types of businesses

- Private individuals

- Self

Where Are the Jobs?

Web developers may be self-employed or work for someone else. Those who work for companies generally work in climate-controlled offices—in fact, job sites tend to be a little chilly, since computer equipment has to be kept from overheating. Web development is not a very physically active occupation and involves sitting in front of a computer for long stretches of time. This does not mean the job is not without its risks, though: like all workers who use computers for long periods of time, Web developers often complain of eyestrain, back problems, and joint problems, such as carpal tunnel syndrome. Of course, if you are a freelance Web developer, you can do your work on a laptop while sitting in an air-conditioned café or on a park bench on a sunny day.

Hours vary widely. Though a 40-hour week is standard, Web developers may work long hours on projects. This is because of the need to meet deadlines, the general culture of the industry, and individual personalities—Web developers tend to be perfectionists. Freelancers tend to work irregularly. They may have more work than they can handle one week, and little the next.

▲ One perk of being a Web developer is choosing your own hours and workplace. You can work at an office with your peers or you can work alone at home with no 9–5 restrictions.

A Typical Day

Here are the highlights of a typical day for a Web developer.

Meet and greet. Your company has been hired to do the Web site for a clothing company's new product line. Before beginning the project, though, you have to organize. Some people will handle the graphics, while some will handle the programming.

See a typical day in the life of a Web developer.

Do a mockup. Back at your desk, you quickly translate some ideas into HTML code. Soon you have a working model of how the site will look.

Back to the drawing board. The site is presented to the client later that afternoon, and they offer their critiques. Unfortunately, they want a complete revision. You'll be working on follow-up changes all day tomorrow. This is going to be a long project!

Start Preparing Now

- Learn HTML, Flash, PHP, and everything else you need to know for the job.

- Create Web sites of your own using these technologies to show prospective clients and employers.

- Network with professionals in the field. They can help to get your work seen.

Training and How to Get It

There is no one career path for entering the world of Web development. While there are schools, courses, and certificate programs, these are not, strictly speaking, necessary. What is more important is that a designer can do good work, understands the technology, and (in large companies) cooperates with others. To this end, work experience matters more than education. See "Finding a Job," below, for tips on how to gain experience.

NOTES FROM THE FIELD

Web developer, Berkeley, California

Q: *How did you get your job?*

A: I created a humor site with friends who wanted an unfiltered voice on the Web. It wasn't really sophisticated or pretty, or for that matter really funny, but it did help me establish credentials for getting my current job.

Q: *What do you like best about your job?*

A: I just like making Web sites. You have an idea, develop your content, design a Web site to present it, and there it is! You can instantly get your ideas in people's faces. Especially with my own site, I liked control, being "the decider" of what appears.

Q: *What's the most challenging part of your job?*

A: The challenge is what makes it rewarding, I guess. I like creating the content, but maintaining and updating a Web site can be rather time consuming and eventually tedious. That's why I stopped updating my original site. It's a lot easier if you're getting paid for it!

Q: *What are the keys to success as a Web developer?*

A: The key to success is persistence. For about four years we continually updated the site, developed new content, made friends via boards and Web associations, which led to more and more links from quality sites. Basically, we had something going for us, but it took a lot of work for people to know we even existed—but once they did, traffic shot up.

Many programmers and Web developers learn the technical aspects on their own. There are books that teach the elements, which many find very useful. There are also online tutorials that you can use. Other aspiring Web developers ask questions on Internet message boards, learning from more experienced programmers and designers. One way to start is to simply click on "view" and then "page source" (or just hit "Ctrl" and "U") when viewing a Web page.

▲ Learning to write and read code is an essential skill for Web developers.

This will show you the HTML code for the page. Download it to your own computer, take it, and play with it.

Most important is a good sense of design. Nobody likes a site in garish colors with blinking text and crude graphics (except, perhaps, as a joke). Look at sites you like and try to imitate them. Experiment with different color schemes and layouts. Meanwhile, pay attention in computer, math, and art classes, as these will serve you well later.

Learn the Lingo

Here are a few words you'll hear as a Web developer:

- **WYSIWYG** "what you see is what you get," the generic name for a program that designs Web pages. You can graphically manipulate the parts of the page, such as text and images, on-screen, and it will automatically generate the code. Unfortunately, the code is not always as "clean" and elegant as a hand-coded Web site.

- **PHP** Personal Home Page tools, a way of creating dynamic and quickly-changing content. A PHP-driven Web site can, for instance, fit articles coded in PHP format into a generic template.

- **Flash** A program published by Adobe that adds animation and interactivity to Web sites.

Finding a Job

Perhaps the easiest way to get started in Web development is to simply ask someone, "Can I design a Web site for you?" In order to get work, it helps to have a portfolio of sites that you've created. This not only shows your talents, but will help you compete against applicants with more education by showing that you can actually do the job.

If you want to be a freelance Web developer, you can find clients by sending out flyers and letters to local businesses, hanging flyers, and other direct methods. You should also post on online message boards such as Craigslist (www.craigslist.org) and check job listings at sites like Monster (www.monster.com) and, of course, create a Web page of your own for clients to see! Word of mouth is very important in this field: if you are good at what you do, old clients will recommend you to new ones.

In order to find opportunities at already existing businesses, look in the local newspaper and especially in online job boards. Also ask people who work in the industry. Very often, they will know if local companies are hiring.

Tips for Success

- Pay attention to a client's wishes—but also know when what they want is impractical or not suited to their needs.

- Keep on top of new technology. The Web is changing every day, and more and more features are being added.

Reality Check

While Web development is interesting and creative work, you will be competing in the job market against people with college degrees. Be sure your work is better than theirs!

Related Jobs to Consider

Computer support specialist. If you're good at fixing computer problems, why not do it for a living?

Computer network technician. Set up and repair computer systems.

Graphic production technician. Create graphics without having to learn computer coding.

LEARN MORE ONLINE

DEVLOUNGE
Useful community site for Web developers.
http://www.devlounge.net

DESIGNERSTALK
Another valuable community site. http://www.designerstalk.com/forums

USABILITY 101
Explanation of the concept from usability guru Jakob Nielsen. https://www.nngroup.com/articles/usability-101-introduction-to-usability/

How to Move Up

- Learn more. The more you can do, the better your job opportunities.

- Start your own business. If you have a lot of clients, why not go into business for yourself?

- Become a programmer. Go back to school or get your certification to work on the "back end."

TEXT-DEPENDENT QUESTIONS

1. *What are some of the languages and software you should understand to be a Web developer?*

2. *What are some specific tasks that Web designers must perform?*

3. *What are some tips to succeeding in this field?*

RESEARCH PROJECTS

1. *Get to work making a portfolio. Talk to friends and family to see who needs a Web site and offer to create it for them. Then seek feedback from others on your site and how well it works or how it could be better.*

2. *Start learning HTML. There are a number of sites that you can use to teach yourself HTML for free, such as Solo Learn. https://www.sololearn.com/Course/HTML/*

▲ Although much of a Web developer's time is spent working alone, you will also need to listen to and address a client's needs and feedback.

Computer Network Technician

9

Learn to build and maintain computer networks. Work with the latest technologies. Enjoy job stability.

WORDS TO UNDERSTAND

certification: a document testifying that someone has obtained a particular level of training.

cybersecurity: the practices and technologies that protect computer networks from attack by hackers or viruses.

telecommunications: the technology sector focused on communications.

With the increasing computerization of the workforce, many specialized and very important jobs have emerged to help organize and maintain companies' computer resources. Computer network technicians build, maintain, and operate networks—systems by which computers share information and access e-mail. Without these computer networks, many companies' ability to do business would grind to a halt. Essentially, any organization with more than one employee has at least some level of need for computer networking. Everything from hospitals and school systems to your library and local Wal-Mart all depend on their computer systems to function. Since the main qualification for the job is obtaining and maintaining certificates to run a variety of server applications, being a computer network technician is a very lucrative and stable career you can begin without having to go to college.

◄ When something goes wrong in a large computer system, network technicians are the best people to solve the problem.

Is This Job Right for You?

To find out if being a computer network technician is right for you, read each of the following questions and answer "Yes" or "No."

Yes	*No*	**1.**	*Are you a good problem solver?*
Yes	*No*	**2.**	*Are you good with computers?*
Yes	*No*	**3.**	*Can you work as part of a team?*
Yes	*No*	**4.**	*Are you very patient?*
Yes	*No*	**5.**	*Do you have good written and spoken communication skills?*
Yes	*No*	**6.**	*Do you like to work indoors in an office environment?*
Yes	*No*	**7.**	*Are you good at both giving and following directions?*
Yes	*No*	**8.**	*Do you stay calm in high-stress situations?*
Yes	*No*	**9.**	*Can you understand and process complex problems?*
Yes	*No*	**10.**	*Do you like helping people?*

If you answered "Yes" to most of these questions, you might be right for a career as a computer network technician. To find out more about this job, read on.

What's the Work Like?

Computer network technicians are in charge of building, maintaining, and supporting computer networks—that is, workers' personal computers that are linked, either wirelessly or by fiber-optic cables, to *servers*. Servers are powerful central computers that store and deliver computer files to users' computers as they are needed. There are several different companies that manufacture servers, all of which program their machines to work slightly differently. A computer network technician may know how to work with one or more of these systems.

A network has capabilities beyond simply serving files, of course. It may be used for **telecommunications**, such as Voice over Internet Protocol (VoIP). It is

TALKING MONEY

The U.S. Department of Labor uses a slightly different term to describe this job: computer network support specialist. The median income is $67,770, but the pay can vary between $37,100 and $91,300. According to Robert Half International, starting salaries range from around $37,000 to $106,000. Those with more education tend to be higher earners.

▲ A computer network specialist needs to know all about the latest computer viruses.

also how a company connects its workers to the Internet. You may be in charge of maintaining security features such as *filters,* which prevent users from accessing certain Web sites, or *firewalls,* which prevent intruders from getting into your company's computers. There are also routine tasks, such as giving new employees access to the network and backing up files. **Cybersecurity** is a constant focus of everyone who works in computer networking.

TALKING TRENDS

Because of the ever-increasing importance of computers in the economy and companies' interest in securing their networks, the number of computer network technicians will continue growing. Because computer network technicians must be present on-site, the career is fairly well insulated from offshoring, or moving call centers to foreign countries where people speak English but wages are much lower.

Who's Hiring?

- Private businesses of all kinds

- Government agencies

- Hospitals and other health care businesses

- Public and private schools, kindergarten through 12th grade

- Colleges and universities

Where Are the Jobs?

Computer network technicians usually work in comfortable, well-lit offices and computer labs. Since computers require air-conditioning to keep them from overheating, offices tend to be a little chilly. Though some physical labor is required, such as lifting, moving, and installing new computers, the computer network technician's job tends to be sedentary. When computer network technicians find themselves gaining weight, many blame their job! Also, like all workers who use computers for long stretches of time, computer network technicians are at risk for eyestrain, back problems, and joint problems, such as carpel tunnel syndrome. Regular exercise helps to prevent these problems. Because companies may have customers all over the world in different time zones or employees who work odd hours, computer network technicians may have to work night or weekend shifts. They may also need to put in overtime during crises, such as system crashes, or when performing upgrades, since this is usually done during off-hours so as not to interfere with users' work.

The size of a computer network technician's office may have no relation to the size of the organization. A university may only have a few computer network technicians on call for hundreds or thousands of users, while a relatively small software company may maintain a sizable staff. A computer network technician's workload varies widely: One day you may only need to assign a username to a new employee, while the next, the entire system may come crashing down.

Start Preparing Now

- Learn everything you can. Potential employers will want to know that you know computer systems.

▲ Malicious viruses are the most serious challenge facing computer network technicians.

- Enroll in a training course to obtain **certification**.

- If you can, get specialized training in cybersecurity. This will increase your attractiveness to an employer.

A Typical Day

Here are the highlights of a typical day for a computer network technician working for a large corporation.

A few administrative tasks. The day starts with a few normal duties—creating network accounts for new employees, checking to make sure the night shift backed up the servers, and the usual paperwork.

All of a sudden . . . The call comes in: One of the servers has gone down. Hundreds of workers can't get to their files. The network technician staff springs into action.

NOTES FROM THE FIELD

Computer network technician, New York, New York

Q: *How did you get your job?*

A: I was offered a part-time, night-shift position at a hospital from a project manager whom I've worked with in the past. He happens to be the information technology operations manager at that same facility. I watch the servers to make sure nothing crashes and back up the files.

Q: *What do you like best about your job?*

A: The night shift is quiet, and since I'm also going to school while I work, I can study during downtime when there aren't any computer users to attend to.

Q: *What's the most challenging part of your job?*

A: The challenging part is the backing up of various application servers during the night. I like doing that, though.

Q: *What are the keys to success as a computer network technician?*

A: One must listen and follow up on the requested needs of clients and supervisors. Positive work relationships ought to be cultivated with your peers, thereby solidifying potential work contacts and references for the future. Finally, the value of the suggestions you put forth toward solving a perceived problem displays initiative and flexible thinking.

Problem resolved. After some diagnostics and searching, you trace the problem to a burned-out motherboard in one of the servers. You quickly swap the broken board for a new one and reboot the system. Once again the day is saved, thanks to the computer network technician. To wind down, you spend a few hours after lunch learning the ins and outs of a new scheduling program management is thinking about deploying company-wide, but which you need to check out first.

◀ A computer network technician analyzes a server to diagnose an issue.

Learn the Lingo

Here are a few words you'll hear as a computer network technician:

- **Firewall** The security barrier between a company's network and the outside world.

- **Server** A central computer that provides services to other computers. They can also act as storage spaces for data.

- **Network** Many computers linked together by fiber-optic cables and servers.

Training and How to Get It

Though a college degree is not always necessary to work as a computer network technician, many colleges and technical schools offer courses toward certification as a computer network technician. This usually includes basic electronic theory and instruction toward a certification exam. Computer network technicians are also sometimes trained by the companies that employ them, especially if they begin at the bottom, for instance as a support specialist. Another venue for training is the armed forces. The navy, for instance, makes great use of computer network technicians (where they are known as information systems technicians). Training will usually include familiarization with the various servers, systems, and procedures.

Servers run on several different operating systems. In order to have the best employment opportunities, you must pass a certification exam for a specific operating system, such as Microsoft, Sun, Cisco, or Red Hat (for Linux). Of these, the best-known is the Mi-

Here is a video with more information about getting trained as a computer network technician.

crosoft Certified Systems Engineer, or MCSE. The exams cost $125 to $150 to take. Upon passing, students are considered qualified to build and maintain computer systems using that operating system. You can find many self-study books for these exams in libraries, bookstores, and online. There are also courses you can take to prepare for the exam.

Finding a Job

Because people in the computer network technician field are used to computers and the Internet, companies often place help-wanted ads on job-search sites like Monster (http://www.monster.com). Another method for finding a job is asking friends and relatives who work in network engineering or technical support. They may be aware of an entry-level opening at their companies or one with which they work. While the best-paid jobs are in large, geographically central, or technology-driven cities, such as New York, Toronto, Chicago, and Seattle, computer network technicians are in great demand in all sorts of businesses, especially those that deal with data and information. Make sure that your certifications are up-to-date and that your references and letters of recommendation emphasize your skill with computers. Also make sure your résumé includes all the computer-related jobs that you have had. If you are looking for experience, consider an unpaid internship or even beginning as a computer support specialist. Though your total related experience can help, it is also important that you show a potential employer that you are eager to learn. Think about what would make you right for the job, develop your skills, and be positive.

Tips for Success

- Know everything you can about whatever technology you use in your job, and stay on top of updates and changes. Technology evolves quickly, and computer professionals can never stop learning .

- Machines are just an important part of the job. How you deal with people, and how well you understand their needs, will significantly determine your success.

Reality Check

Being a computer network technician can be frustrating. Many people don't understand how networks and systems work—and they expect you to go along with their ill-informed ideas.

Related Jobs to Consider

Computer support specialist. Why not begin in technical support while studying for your certification?

AutoCAD technician, graphic production technician. These computer workers do not necessarily need advanced certification—just know-how.

Computer programmer. Many computer programmers are self-taught. If you are a skilled programmer, you can get a well-paying job making programs or games. If you are qualified to be a network technician, you may also easily be able to become a programmer!

How to Move Up

- Get that certification! Not only does it mean more money, it will open doors to advancement.

- Keep learning. Many employers like to see a two- or four-year degree for higher-level employees, or even that you're working toward one. You may find your local institution has favorable financial aid policies for working students, and that they give credit for work experience. Computer network technicians enjoy great upward mobility and are often promoted based more on their performance in their jobs than their education. At the top levels, computer network technicians may help create an organization's information-technology policies.

- Be persistent. Because the computer industry is changing so rapidly, formal training other than certification classes is of limited use. Many computer support specialists learn enough "on the job" to move up. In time, you may become a supervisor or administrator.

LEARN MORE ONLINE

COMPTIA
Check out the site of a top network certification company. https://certification.comptia.org/certifications/network

MICROSOFT CERTIFIED SYSTEMS ENGINEER
Microsoft's page on becoming a Certified systems engineer. https://www.microsoft.com/en-us/learning/mcse-certification.aspx

TEXT-DEPENDENT QUESTIONS

1. *What are some of the operating systems a technician might need to understand?*

2. *What are some keys to success in this field?*

3. *What is certification and why is it so important?*

RESEARCH PROJECTS

1. *Explore the free training pages at Microsoft: https://mva.microsoft.com/. Consider registering for Microsoft's "Virtual Academy" to learn about game development, mobile apps, and much more.*

2. *Try taking baby steps toward this career by offering to help with network maintenance at your home, school, or other places. Pay attention to how you feel about the experience: Do you enjoy helping people with their technical issues?*

INDEX

PHOTO CREDITS

Cover
(Central image) Shutterstock/Burlingham; (top to bottom) Shutterstock/wavebreakmedia, iStock/philipimage, Shutterstock/guruXOX, iStock/amriphoto, Shutterstock/ESB Professional

Interior
4 (left to right), Shutterstock/wavebreakmedia; iStock/philipimage; Shutterstock/ESB Professional; Shutterstock/guruXOX; iStock/amriphoto; 7, iStock/laflor; 8, Shutterstock/guruXOX; 11, iStock/guruXOOX; 12, Shutterstock/DW labs Incorporated; 13 (top), iStock/recep-bg; 13 (bottom), Shutterstock/Soloviov Vadym; 16, Shutterstock/Gorodenkoff; 20, Shutterstock/Oleksandr Nagaiets; 22, iStock/bjones27; 24, Shutterstock/Corepics VOF; 25, iStock/surfleader; 27, iStock/bjones27; 30, iStock/KatarzynaBialasiewicz; 33, iStock/NicolasMcComber; 34, Shutterstock/Volodymyr Burdiak; 35, Shutterstock/guruXOX; 37, Shutterstock/luanateutzi; 42, iStock/recep-bg; 45, iStockGrassetto; 46, iStock/pkfawcett; 48, Shutterstock/thanatphoto; 51, iStock/leezsnow; 53, Shutterstock/Andrey_Popov; 54, Shutterstock/Burlingham; 57, Shutterstock/Andrey_Popov; 58, iStock/Bojan89; 59, Shutterstock/Golubovy; 61, Shutterstock/wavebreakmedia; 66, iStock/Jason_V; 69, iStock/alex-mit; 71, Shutterstock/alphaspirit; 71, Shutterstock/alphaspirit; 72, iStock/peshkov; 76, Shutterstock/Anna Mente; 79 (top), Shutterstock/Lia Koltyrina; 79 (bottom), Shutterstock/Anton_Ivanov; 81, Shutterstock/Lauren Elisabeth; 87, iStock/SetsukoN; 88, Shutterstock/ProStockStudio; 91, Shutterstock/Rawpixel.com; 92, Shutterstock/Rawpixel.com; 93, Shutterstock/ESB Professional; 96, Shutterstock/crazydanger; 99, iStock/Yuri_Arcurs; 100, Shutterstock/wavebreakmedia; 103, Shutterstock/Rawpixel.com; 105, iStock/drxy; 107, Shutterstock/wavebreakmedia